Graduate Entrepreneurship

Also by Michael Tefula:

Student Procrastination: Seize the Day and Get More Work Done
How to Get a First: Insights and Advice from a First-class Graduate

Graduate Entrepreneurship

How to Start Your Business after University

Michael Tefula

 macmillan education   palgrave

First published 2017 by
PALGRAVE

Palgrave in the UK is an imprint of Macmillan Publishers Limited, registered in England, company number 785998, of 4 Crinan Street, London, N1 9XW.

Palgrave Macmillan in the US is a division of St Martin's Press LLC, 175 Fifth Avenue, New York, NY 10010.

Palgrave is a global imprint of the above companies and is represented throughout the world.

Palgrave® and Macmillan® are registered trademarks in the United States, the United Kingdom, Europe and other countries.

ISBN 978–1–137–49317–0 paperback

This book is printed on paper suitable for recycling and made from fully managed and sustained forest sources. Logging, pulping and manufacturing processes are expected to conform to the environmental regulations of the country of origin.

A catalogue record for this book is available from the British Library.

A catalog record for this book is available from the Library of Congress.

Printed and bound by CPI Group (UK) Ltd, Croydon, CR0 4YY

Contents

List of figures and tables

Figures

Tables

Preface

This book is the culmination of a journey that goes back to the first time I made money from something entrepreneurial. Back then I had no idea what entrepreneurship was; I was still in secondary school and had no particular interest in business. But over the years I developed an ear for music and took part in music production in my spare time. Thanks to the Internet it wasn't long before I was selling musical instrumentals to aspiring artists online.

As I reflect back on those years I can see that I mostly had no clue about business. However, I did three good things that are typical of most entrepreneurs:

- I spotted an opportunity to make money.
- I quickly worked out whether it would be worth my effort.
- I then learnt enough about the Internet to use it as a tool to find and engage with potential customers.

This early venture turned out to be a modest success: I was lucky enough to make a few thousand pounds through an activity I considered a hobby. More importantly, this venture opened my eyes to the power of creativity and business – two things I've been fascinated by ever since.

I am now a professional working adult but continue to exercise the entrepreneurial muscles I discovered in my early teens. In effect I strive to have an entrepreneurial mindset in everything that I do. And thanks to this mindset I was able to start a t-shirt business and content marketing venture while at university; I was able to co-found a niche restaurant during a personal sabbatical; and in terms of employment, an entrepreneurial mindset helped me secure job opportunities at the likes of Deloitte (one of the largest consulting firms in the world), BGF (a £2.5bn investment fund), and Palgrave (my publisher).

An entrepreneurial mindset has opened a lot of doors for me and I hope that with this book it will open many doors for you too. So as you read on remember this: being entrepreneurial isn't just about starting a business; it's about being proactive enough to take advantage of opportunities that can transform your life.

Michael Tefula
June 2016

Acknowledgements

Writing never gets easier but I've been blessed to make it a part of a fulfilling career, not least because of the amazing support from my family and friends.

I am forever indebted to my parents, Moses and Barbara Tefula, whose unwavering support and inspiration got me to where I am today. I could not have asked for better role models and I count myself lucky to have them as parents. I am also thankful to my brothers, Mark, Benjamin, Simon, and Brian, for their counsel, good cheer, and encouragement.

In addition to my family, I'd like to extend gratitude to Nikita Thakrar, who is a friend who is as rare as they come. She's the first person I call whenever I need to talk through start-up ideas, but in many ways she's also the sister I never had. Thank you for putting up with my endless calls and questions, Niki.

It goes without saying that *Graduate Entrepreneurship* is the result of hundreds of conversations. Many individuals helped me refine the ideas in this book. Stacey Barnes, Martin Phillips, Arthur Wamala, Emily Braybrook, as well as all the wonderful entrepreneurs I interviewed for this title, thank you for your insights and advice.

Finally I would like to extend a warm thank you to Helen Caunce and the team at Palgrave. You did a stellar job helping me put the book together and I am deeply grateful for your efforts.

Introduction

There's never been a better time to start a business. The barriers to starting a venture are lower than ever thanks to technology, the Internet, and the proliferation of business knowledge and education. Not only that but public and private sectors in many developed countries are doing more to support local entrepreneurs. For example, at the time of writing the UK government offers low-interest loans to entrepreneurs through delivery partners like *Virgin StartUp*, who also offer mentoring services. The private sector has also chimed in: at the time of writing *Natwest* and *KPMG* are backers of *Entrepreneurial Spark,* a non-profit organisation that provides free office space and mentoring to all types of entrepreneurs.

Many of these amenities take the pain out of starting a business and it would be a shame not to use them if you've ever pondered starting a venture of your own. However, in order to make the most of an environment and a period that is increasingly favourable to entrepreneurs you have to be willing to start something. You need to have a business idea and you need the courage to develop and pursue it. This book aims to get you off the ground in this regard. It's a starting point but certainly not the end of your entrepreneurship journey.

In this book you will learn enough about entrepreneurship to be able to set off on a path of your own for further learning. In a moment we will touch on what's to come in the rest of the book, but before we get to that there are four important points to keep in mind.

1. The graduate advantage

If you have already graduated from university, congratulations – you have an advantage. Data shows that the average business founded by a university graduate generates 25 percent more revenue than the average company founded by a high school dropout.[1] Of course, this advantage is not driven by merely having a degree. It's driven by the knowledge and networks you accumulate during your studies. Furthermore, if you are already employed, your professional experience can also be a great asset when you start a business.

2. The weird and wonderful nature of entrepreneurship

There are many books on entrepreneurship but don't let that convince you that it is an exact science. Entrepreneurship is more of an art. You can learn all the technical chops but they don't guarantee you a hit. This is because the environments in which entrepreneurs start businesses vary from person to person. The technology, economy, founding teams, consumer sentiments, availability of funding, potency of the competition, and government legislation all play a part in defining the success of a venture. And in some ways luck (or perhaps fortuitous timing) plays a role in all success stories. Regardless, just as a painter or musician can master the skills necessary to capitalise on moments of inspiration, an entrepreneur can also hone a number of basic principles that enable him or her to make the most of an economic opportunity. And it is such principles and fundamental ideas that will be the focus of this book.

3. Entrepreneurship requires real-world practice

This book is a great place to start but it's important to appreciate that the best lessons about business happen in business. Entrepreneurship can't be learnt with just a book. You have to take the ideas suggested in the following chapters and put them to practice in the real world. That's where you will get feedback on your efforts and that's where you will be able to tell what works for you and what doesn't.

4. Entrepreneurship skills are also valuable to employees

In this book you will learn the basics of entrepreneurship. But being entrepreneurial isn't just about starting a business. If you currently work at a professional firm you will notice that the more senior you get the more entrepreneurial you have to be. Partners in consulting firms, for example, have to go out and win new clients in order to grow their firms. Imagine what kind of advantage you would have as a manager if you had a string of entrepreneurial experiences behind you and a knack for spotting opportunities, selling, strategy, marketing, and sales.

Who this book is for

So who was this book written for? It's mainly written for students and graduates who are thinking about starting a business, particularly those who are concerned by any of the following:

- I don't have any good business ideas.
- I'm worried about the risks involved.
- I have a full-time job and can't commit yet.
- What if I fail?
- I don't have enough money.
- I have no business experience.
- I'm too young (or too old).
- I don't know where to start.

All of these concerns will be addressed throughout this book.

What you'll get from the book

Before everything else, you will first learn about the realities of entrepreneurship and what it involves. After that the book is split into three parts.

The first part of the book deals with the entrepreneurial mindset and in this section you will:

- Develop the confidence required to start a business.
- Learn about passion and how to cultivate it.
- Appreciate the value of persevering in business.

- Find tips on how to be more creative.
- Get an overview of what leadership is and what it means for entrepreneurs.

The second part of the book addresses five fundamental skills every entrepreneur should have. You will learn about:

- Strategy
- Marketing
- Sales
- Branding
- Finance

This list is by no means exhaustive but it will get you off to a good start.

The final section of the book guides you on the practical aspects of starting a business. You will:

- Learn how and where to find business ideas.
- Obtain rules of thumb to help you evaluate opportunities.
- Use a seven-step process to kick-start your venture.

Throughout the book you will also come across a number of useful features to supplement your reading. These are:

- Insight Boxes – Experiences from real-world entrepreneurs, many of whom were interviewed specifically for this book.
- Tip Boxes – Actionable entrepreneurship tips you can use right away.
- Food for Thought – A break from the main text and a chance to reflect on related ideas.
- Reflection Areas – Positioned at the end of a chapter to help you practise concepts from the chapter.
- Useful Resources – References to books, movies, and links that you will find useful in your journey to start a business.
- Notes – A place for you to jot down any ideas you may have as you read along.

How to read this book

You can read this book in one sitting or over several days. You can read it with a friend who's thinking about starting a business or you can read it on your own. Whatever approach you take, be sure to scribble down lots of thoughts as you go along because entrepreneurship is about ideas. Furthermore, aim to make something happen in the real world because entrepreneurship is also about action.

The seven myths of entrepreneurship

What you will gain from this chapter:

1. Learn about the realities of entrepreneurship.
2. Question the assumptions you may take for granted.
3. Eliminate fears about starting a business.

Myth 1: You need a great idea

Everyone has a business idea in them but they never think it's good enough. This is because people often judge early ideas against already established businesses. However, no venture ever starts fully formed. Every successful idea starts small and over time can mature into greatness. Did you know, for example, that Sir Richard Branson's *Virgin Group* started as a small mail-ordering business? The company would take orders through the post and mail music records to customers. In those early days it is doubtful Branson knew how big his venture would become.

The reality of entrepreneurship is that an idea does not have to be perfect from the get-go; nor does it have to be extraordinary. For instance, in a survey that involved 100 highly revered start-ups only 12 percent of the founders attributed their success to an extraordinary or unusual idea. The other 88 percent attributed most of their success to the *extraordinary* execution of an *ordinary* idea.[1]

In light of the above, the pressure we place on ourselves to come up with a revolutionary idea is unjustified. Few successful businesses ever start that way and many great entrepreneurs simply execute an existing idea better than everyone else has done. In other words, you don't need a great idea to start a business. You just need a reasonable concept to build upon.

Myth 2: Entrepreneurs are born not made

The founder of *Nike*, Phil Knight, did not realise he wanted to be an entrepreneur until he got into business school for his master's. It was during a class when a lecturer asked students to invent a new business that Phil realised that's exactly what he wanted to do as a profession.[2] Was Phil Knight born an entrepreneur? No. He didn't pursue the craft until his later years. Moreover, this is just one example among many where someone becomes an entrepreneur but it wasn't always something they had a natural inclination towards. And yet the myth that entrepreneurs are born lives on.

The truth is there's no evidence that some people are natural-born entrepreneurs while others are not. Research indicates that entrepreneurs come from both entrepreneurial and non-entrepreneurial families. In one survey, which involved more than 500 company founders, more than half of the people surveyed (52 percent) were the first in their families to launch a business.[3] If entrepreneurship is genetic you would not expect this percentage to be so high. And so the conclusion is clear: you aren't born an entrepreneur; you become one.

Myth 3: Age matters

Web entrepreneur and YouTube personality Zoe 'Zoella' Sugg was in her early twenties when she started to earn a reported £20,000 a month from her social media ventures.[4] Fraser Doherty set up his jam-making business when he was just 14 and, by the time he was 18, he was supplying jam to the supermarket chain *Waitrose*. There's no shortage of media coverage on young entrepreneurs because the younger they are, the more sensational the story. But these reports warp our view on the relationship between age and entrepreneurship. The reality is far more diverse.

Doris Fisher co-founded *Gap* when she was 37 years old. Ruth Handler launched the *Barbie* dolls business aged 42. Giorgio Armani didn't start his company until he was 41. And a 55-year-old pharmacist invented *Coca-Cola*. Most entrepreneurs actually start a business in their late thirties to mid-forties. In fact, the average age for a first-time founder is 45.[5] The media, however, finds younger entrepreneurs more newsworthy so you'll always hear more about the twenty-something millionaire and less about the mature businessperson.

Does this mean that you should wait until you are 35–45 years old to start a business? Not necessarily. Starting a business when you are young has advantages. You have fewer responsibilities and can be more flexible. On the other hand, when you're older you may have a mortgage and family to think about and that restricts the sort of risks you can take. The flipside, of course, is that you will have more experience, a better network of contacts, and perhaps even more cash to invest. Each age group has its pros and cons but a major advantage to starting now is the flexibility and energy that comes with youth.

Myth 4: Entrepreneurs love risk

Another common misconception is that entrepreneurs love risk and that you have to be a big risk-taker to become an entrepreneur. However, when it comes to risk preferences business owners aren't that much different from the general public. If you asked an entrepreneur to leave their car unlocked while shopping they would view the risk of theft to be just as high as anyone else's assessment. There's a possible key difference, however: entrepreneurs are generally more confident and optimistic. When reviewing a business opportunity they have a strong belief in their ability to profit from a venture. In contrast, other people are likely to see threats where entrepreneurs see opportunity.[6] On that account, entrepreneurs are not risk-taking enthusiasts. They simply believe that if they work effectively they can turn risk into reward.

Myth 5: Nine out of ten businesses fail

One of the most common myths in entrepreneurship is that nine out of ten businesses fail. Fortunately, the statistic is an exaggeration. It's too simplistic and ignores a component that, if removed, leads us to forget an even more bizarre reality: over a long enough timeline all businesses come to an end. A vivid example of this phenomenon is that of the world's oldest business, the Japanese company *Kongō Gumi*. After running for an impressive 1,400 years the company ended in 2006[7] – an impressive run, no doubt, since the average life span of a company is 40–50 years.[8]

The ultimate end of all businesses, which by the way should not worry you, given the timespans involved, highlights an important point: when we talk about business failure rates we also have to consider a time component. A more telling statistic should tell us how many businesses fail over a specified period of time. Fortunately, this data is available and it is more encouraging than the usual nine-out-of-ten-businesses-fail mantra (see Figure 1.1).

Figure 1.1: Data from research on survival chances of new businesses.[10]

According to a study by researchers from the University of Sussex and *Barclays Bank*, only one in six businesses (16.98 percent) fail in the first year. Over time this proportion increases, but even after six years, 30 percent of the original companies are still running.[9] So next time someone tells you that nine out of ten businesses fail, ask them, 'after how many years?'

With that said, it's worth acknowledging that statistics are informative but not always instructive. Taken alone, the above numbers tell you nothing about the kind of things you can do to enhance your chances of success (more on this in Part 3). The numbers reflect a select group of businesses that might be completely different from your venture. As such, don't assume that your fate has already been sealed. Your chances are better than you think!

⌘ Investor's Insight
Vinod Kholsa, founder of *Kholsa Ventures*

The business of investing in companies is risky because only a few make it. But billionaire investor Vinod Kholsa sees it another way: a 90 percent failure rate is not discouraging if you have a 10 percent chance of making 100 times your money.[11] Bold entrepreneurs don't concern themselves with how poor the odds are. Instead, they envision success and focus on making it real.

Myth 6: Starting a business is straightforward

Few people believe that starting a business is easy but many underestimate the effort it takes. Entrepreneurs generally work longer hours and at the early stage of a venture don't get paid much. According to research from the UK, entrepreneurs work an average of 52 hours a week. That's 63 percent longer than traditional employees.[12] In America the renowned investor David Rose says he has never met an entrepreneur who works fewer than 60 hours a week. He believes that starting a business is an 'all-in sport'.[13] You can't do things half-heartedly. Once the engine gets going you have to commit fully (more on this in Chapter 15).

In addition to the long hours there's usually little to no salary in the early stages of a venture. The founders of *Innocent Drinks*, for example, didn't have any income for 12 months. It took them four years before they could earn a salary of £40,000, which was the same amount they had left at their corporate jobs.[14]

Paradoxically, entrepreneurs are happier than most people are. In a global survey of over 197,000 individuals, authors of the *2013 Global Entrepreneurship Monitor Report*[15] found that entrepreneurs score higher on ratings of happiness and life satisfaction when compared to non-entrepreneurs. So while it's harder to start a business it's also often more satisfying than regular employment. You enjoy more creative freedom and the hours fly by when you're working on something you really care about.

Myth 7: You need lots of money

You don't always need a lot of money to start. The amount of cash you will need depends on the type of business you hope to start. For instance, there are many examples of people who started an online business for less than £100 but went on to make six-figure incomes.[16] On the other hand, a small coffee shop that seats about 20 people might cost you between £15,000 and £20,000 to set up.

The general pattern is that service companies have lower costs while product-based businesses (restaurants, manufacturers, retailers) tend to have higher costs. Regardless, in Chapter 15 we will look at some of the ways you can start with a minimal amount of resources.

As a side note it's worth pointing out that there is a danger to having too much money at the start of a venture. You may be tempted to spend money on every problem. For example, if you aren't generating enough sales you might be inclined to spend more money on marketing even if the product is not satisfying customers. In contrast, being short on resources instils a stricter discipline. You are forced to consider the underlying issues as to why something isn't working, instead of using the brute force of cash to attack every problem.

The truth about entrepreneurship

You may have never considered entrepreneurship until now. You may still be at university, or you may be a graduate. Regardless of your current position it's never too late to start a business. The odds of success – especially if you are educated – are better than most people think; you don't need a *million dollar* idea; your age hardly matters; and it's possible to attain the business skills necessary to become an effective entrepreneur. We will return to what these skills are in later chapters but first we need to define entrepreneurship.

Chapter summary

- The statistic that 'nine out of ten businesses fail' is inaccurate. So don't let it put you off.
- You don't need a grand idea to start a business. Many entrepreneurs started with less-sophisticated concepts but went on to develop fantastic businesses.
- The average age for first-time entrepreneurs is 45. But if you start sooner you can take advantage of the flexibility and energy that youth usually brings.
- Starting a business is harder than doing a normal job but entrepreneurs enjoy what they do and many are happier than most people are.
- You don't have to be a big risk taker to be an entrepreneur but you do need to have confidence in your abilities to succeed.
- You don't need lots of money to start a business. In fact, not having a lot of cash will make you more disciplined and frugal.
- Entrepreneurs are made, not born. So you can always cultivate what it takes to become an enterprising individual.

 Reflection

What other impressions do you have about entrepreneurship? What gave you those impressions? How true are they? Are there counterexamples? How have these impressions influenced your thinking?

Spend some time reflecting on the answers to these questions. You might find that some of the ideas you have about entrepreneurship are true, while others are unfounded and are holding you back.

Useful resources

- Video: *The 10 Myths of Entrepreneurship* (2012) by University of St. Gallen (HSG)
  https://youtu.be/G8gRkJ9cnzo

Chapter 1

Why is it worth watching?
It highlights additional myths about entrepreneurship and introduces *the entrepreneurial method,* a theory about entrepreneurship that focuses on entrepreneurs starting with what they already have; choosing business ideas based on what is an acceptable loss; making the most of surprises and uncertainty; and forming partnerships. You can learn more about the entrepreneurial method here: http://www.effectuation.org/learn/effectuation-101

- Book: *The Illusions of Entrepreneurship: The Costly Myths That Entrepreneurs, Investors, and Policy Makers Live By* (2009) by Scott Shane

Why is it worth reading?
This book debunks more than 60 myths about entrepreneurship. It's somewhat academic but worth reading if you'd like to learn more about the economics of self-employment.

What is entrepreneurship?

What you will gain from this chapter:

1. Learn about the origins of commerce.
2. Appreciate the timeless principles of entrepreneurship.
3. Review definitions of entrepreneurship.

A history of enterprise

Why start a chapter with the history of entrepreneurship? There are two reasons. First, history brings to light how old entrepreneurship is. The word 'entrepreneur' may be an 18th century term[1] but entrepreneurs have been around for many thousands of years. Second, by considering the history of enterprise we can identify themes of entrepreneurship that have persisted over the millennia. And though it is true that ancient entrepreneurs had different challenges – for example, primitive technology, crude regulations, and high transport costs – entrepreneurship has elements that have persisted over time.[2] So where did it all start?

The birthplace of entrepreneurship

According to historians the birthplace of enterprise can be traced back to Mesopotamia, a region that lies between Iraq and Iran. This is where the first human civilisation formed and where writing was invented.[3] Mesopotamia was also blessed with fertile land and was rich with agricultural produce. Nonetheless, the region lacked precious metals that could be used for the construction of buildings and weapons. To solve the imbalance public institutions in the region (temples and palaces) turned to local merchants for help: merchants would risk long-distance journeys to export Mesopotamia's produce in exchange for materials that the region lacked. And if the merchants made it back alive they would profit from the venture. As these relationships matured they gave way to commercial practices that we take for granted today. Contracts, money, prices, and markets all came to life some 3,000–5,000 years ago[4] and thanks to such developments, Mesopotamia facilitated the rise of enterprise.

Timeless ideas

Entrepreneurship has been a part of humanity for a very long time but what is just as fascinating is that the fundamentals of the practice haven't changed much. Ancient entrepreneurs in Mesopotamia took dangerous journeys so that they could profit from solving a regional problem. Modern entrepreneurs are no different. They too partake in risky ventures so that they can profit by solving society's problems or fulfilling people's desires. Indeed, the central themes of entrepreneurship – spotting opportunities, assessing potential rewards, managing risks, and co-ordinating efforts – are timeless. Sure, the tactics and environments are always changing, but history tells us that the essence of the craft will remain largely the same.

What a time to be alive

Given the history of entrepreneurship we can count ourselves lucky. We are more educated than ancient traders were and the environment in which we practise entrepreneurship is more favourable. In contrast, merchants in Mesopotamia often risked death during entrepreneurial escapades. Thieves would raid cargoes and wild beasts would pounce on unsuspecting travellers.

> **Key term – Limited Liability:**
> Limited liability applies to incorporated businesses. It means that you can only lose money you have put into a business and no more.

Chapter 2

Today entrepreneurial risks are generally limited to financial losses. And even then, concepts such as limited liability can restrict how much money you can ever lose in a venture. What's more, we now have access to a range of tools that take the pain out of getting started. For example, at the time of writing, you can create a company in the UK within 24 hours through the *Companies House* website. All this can be achieved with just £15 and almost no paperwork.[5] However, just because we have all these advantages today doesn't mean that the fundamental nature of the game has changed, which is why a broad definition of entrepreneurship will be useful.

What is entrepreneurship?

Put simply, entrepreneurship is the process of establishing and running a business. On a more granular level it can be defined as a series of actions that include identifying, evaluating, and exploiting opportunities that create value.[6]

In the business realm, value can be achieved by ventures that tackle social problems, as is the case with social entrepreneurship; ventures that involve political activism, as is the case with political entrepreneurship; or even ventures that involve the preservation and promotion of art and culture, as is the case with cultural entrepreneurship. We will focus on business entrepreneurship in this book. In this category, the value of enterprise is economic in nature. It may involve launching new products, finding and creating new markets, or simply conceiving a better and more profitable way of doing things.[7] (For brevity, we will use the words 'entrepreneurship' and 'business entrepreneurship' synonymously.)

In sum, entrepreneurship is the identification, evaluation, and exploitation of economic opportunities. Therefore, to be an entrepreneur you have to find economic opportunities, assess their worth, and co-ordinate efforts to exploit them. We will return to these steps in Part 3 of the book, but before we get there we will turn to the makings of an entrepreneurial mindset.

Chapter summary

- Entrepreneurship has a rich history that goes back many thousands of years.

Chapter 2

- Even so, entrepreneurs of ancient times aren't all that different from entrepreneurs of today.
- The products, services, and risks of ancient entrepreneurs may be different from those of 21st-century entrepreneurs but the fundamental process of entrepreneurship is the same across time.
- In simple terms, entrepreneurship is the process of establishing and running a business.
- In more concrete terms entrepreneurship is the process of identifying, evaluating, and exploiting economic opportunities.

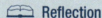 **Reflection**

Can you think of examples in your life where you did the following?

1. Discovered a unique opportunity
2. Evaluated whether an idea was worth pursuing
3. Took steps to make the most of a discovery

Entrepreneurship in this book is about economic opportunities. But if you reflect on your achievements to date you might find examples of where you acted like an entrepreneur even if it didn't involve starting a new company.

Useful resources

- Movie: *Joy* (2015) starring Jennifer Lawrence and Robert De Niro

  Why is it worth watching?
  The movie is loosely based on the colourful life of inventor and entrepreneur Joy Mangano. It includes several entrepreneurship activities such as the discovery of business ideas, pitching for investment, and marketing and selling new products. Jennifer's character also demonstrates many aspects of the entrepreneurial mindset that you will read about in Part 1 of this book.

Mindset

Entrepreneurship is about spotting business opportunities, evaluating their worth, and taking action to exploit them. This process can be highly rewarding but be ready to also have your resolve tested. Starting a business is no piece of cake. You need to develop self-belief, passion, endurance, creativity, and leadership qualities in order to do well. This section of the book will help you to develop each of these attributes. They are part of a mindset that is valuable throughout the process of entrepreneurship.

Self-belief

What you will gain from this chapter:

1. Learn about confidence in entrepreneurship.
2. Understand the value of self-belief.
3. Know how to develop your confidence in business.

Strangely confident

Entrepreneurs have a strange confidence in themselves. It's strange because they're often – at least initially – the only ones who think they can succeed. This characteristic is so prevalent in business leaders that when *PwC*, one of the Big Four accounting firms, surveyed 1,000 CEOs during a global economic slowdown, they reported more than double the confidence in their ability to grow their firms than in the growth prospects of the general economy.[1] This phenomenon is not limited to people who are already successful either.

Though few believed it, a young Warren Buffet always knew he would be wealthy. He rarely doubted himself and was never discouraged in his childhood.[2] Today he's worth more than $70 billion.

Sophia Amoruso, who was once unemployed, broke, and had no sense of direction, recalls in her autobiography how no one would have thought her to be a sure bet in business or in life. This did not discourage her. She bet on herself and eight years later her fashion business *Nasty Gal* generates $100 million in revenue and employs more than 300 staff.[3]

Another example is the Chinese entrepreneur Jack Ma, who failed his university entrance exams twice before being admitted to what was considered his city's worst university. After graduation no one wanted to employ him. Not even *KFC*, who rejected his application to work as a secretary for the restaurant's general manager.[4] Yet Ma never stopped believing that one day he would run his own business. Today he's the head of *Alibaba Group*, a company that's worth more than $200bn.

Despite seemingly unfavourable odds, effective entrepreneurs have a strong sense of self-belief. This confidence directs their efforts and helps them persevere. But what exactly is self-belief? Is it just fluffy positive self-talk or does it have to be substantiated? How can self-belief benefit you? Are people born with it? Can it be developed? This chapter will answer these questions and offer ideas on how you can develop the confidence required to start a successful venture.

 Food for Thought

Self-belief is key if you want to start a business. Without it there is hesitancy and inaction. Even so, it is still surprising how confident some entrepreneurs can be. For instance, in a survey of almost 3,000 new business owners, a third believed that their chance of failure was zero.[5] Such confidence is at odds with reality because more than half of new businesses fail within the first five years. Still, confidence in your ability to do well is more helpful than a doubtful mind. You just have to make sure that confidence (or rather, overconfidence) doesn't blind you from assessing the risks of a venture.

Origins of self-belief

When Fred Smith was a university student he put together an essay about a business idea he had. Upon reading the assignment his management professor offered the following advice:

> 66 The concept is interesting and well formed, but in order to earn better than a 'C', the idea must be feasible.⁶ 99

What would you do in this instance? Would you drop the idea and search for something more realistic? After all, a business professor probably knows more about business than you do. Or would you adopt optimism and continue to develop your concept? Thankfully Fred chose the latter. Had he given up on his idea, the multi-billion dollar company it inspired, *FedEx*, would not exist today.

Such is the power of self-belief. Fred had so much conviction in his idea for overnight deliveries and in his ability to execute it that no expert could stop him from pursuing the venture. But make no mistake; self-belief isn't just about thinking you can do it. It must also be substantiated. If, we look closely at Fred's background we find that like many entrepreneurs, he had several reasons for his conviction, namely:

- Valuable experiences
- Authentic encouragement
- Relevant knowledge and education

Let's see how each of these factors played out in Fred's journey, but as you read them try to think of examples from your own life as well

Experience

Self-confidence is often tied to a history of overcoming challenges and Fred's life was no different. As a young child he had to use crutches due to a birth defect that affected his hips. While this held him back in many ways, he took up the role of managing a baseball team and subsequently won an award for leadership. After he recovered from his ailment Fred played sports, learnt how to fly small aircraft in his teens, excelled academically, and after graduation, served in the army for three years. By the time Fred got into business he was no stranger to beating obstacles. He had a tank full of self-belief and knew that he could achieve anything he set his mind to.

Chapter 3

Food for Thought

Graduate job interviews sometimes include questions such as:

- Tell me about a time you had to overcome an obstacle.
- When did you have to lead a team? How did it go?
- What achievement are you most proud of?

You don't have to answer these questions now but they are worth reflecting on. This is because self-belief thrives when there's evidence of achievement. Indeed, reflecting on your past success – times when you've really had to push yourself to achieve – can help you find the confidence you need to overcome new challenges.

Encouragement

Though developing self-belief is a personal journey, it's never a solitary experience. Friends and family also play a role. For Fred this group included his late father, a businessman who had made his wealth in the transportation industry and the restaurant sector. It also included his uncle, an aviation business owner who gave Fred his first job. Both of these individuals inspired Fred and when it came to challenges in other areas of life, he could count on encouragement from his uncle, sports coaches, teachers, and a distinguished platoon sergeant in the army.[7] But true self-belief doesn't stop here. In Fred's case his conviction was also the result of an education and a careful analysis of the business area he wanted to pursue.

⌘ **Entrepreneur's Insight**
Brigitte West, CEO of *Beauty by the Geeks*

A mentor can be a good source of encouragement when you start your business. (See *Useful Resources* at the end of the chapter for tips on how to find one.) Effective entrepreneurs usually have more than one mentor. Brigitte West, CEO of

Beauty by the Geeks, is a fan of this approach. Here's what she had to say when asked about it:

> *Get some good mentors. Our mentors have been everything –
> whether they're a soundboard or whether they've got great advice.
> We've got a variety of mentors. We don't just have one, we have
> like five, and the reason is that they're all from different industries
> that are relevant to Beauty by the Geeks. We've got some business
> whizzes as mentors – absolutely incredible people; we've also got
> experts in the cosmetics industry. When we've got a problem or want
> to air something, we know which one of our mentors is best to go to.
> And they appreciate that as well.*

Education

Before Fred Smith launched *FedEx* he spent hours learning about the logistics sector. His goal was to make overnight deliveries possible but before he could do that he had to understand why every other courier failed to achieve this aim. This is where education comes in, and not just a university education either. Fred had to engage in self-directed learning and research so he could find a way to overcome inefficiencies in the logistics business.

Fred's research efforts eventually paid off. He crafted a plan for a new business that would use its own aircraft as well as a specialised delivery network. These features helped *FedEx* achieve overnight deliveries and the rest, as they say, is history. By educating himself, Fred not only gained new insights, he also gained the confidence that his idea would work.

What is self-belief?

The Fred Smith story is typical of people who have a strong sense of self-belief. As we have seen, such confidence doesn't come from nothing. Instead, it's driven by:

- A history of achievement or credible experience
- The amount of encouragement you harness
- The knowledge you acquire about your business area.

All these factors contribute to self-belief, which can be defined as the general confidence in your ability to do well. Moreover, self-belief is not just something you are born with. It's possible to develop it and a large body of research shows that it is one of the best predictors of success in a wide range of fields, including, but not limited to, entrepreneurship.[9]

Why you need to believe in yourself

Starting a business can be intimidating to some. Only a few people attempt to start one and even fewer succeed. However, if you can cultivate self-belief you will go further than those who have no faith in their potential. Here are a few reasons why.[10]

Goals

First, self-belief is important because it determines what we choose to do with our lives. If we don't think we'll be good at something, we avoid it. Put another way, if you don't believe you are capable of starting a business, you never will. In contrast, a strong sense of self-belief inspires you to aim higher and helps you to develop capabilities beyond those of less confident people.

Perseverance

Second, people who are confident in their abilities are more resilient. They work harder and rarely give up at the first sign of trouble. A great example is Rowland H. Macy, founder of *Macy's*. Despite failing at four separate retail ventures, he never gave up.[11] Instead, he took lessons from the setbacks and several attempts later established one of America's largest retail groups. Indeed, failure is a natural part of entrepreneurship. But for those who believe in themselves a setback is an opportunity to learn and grow into a more effective entrepreneur.

Personal effectiveness

Finally, people who believe in their ability to do well are able to use their mind more effectively for problem solving and decision-making. Unlike people who have low confidence and who tend to focus on inadequacies, people with high self-belief focus on finding solutions to problems. They approach challenges with less anxiety and do not give in so easily to negative and disruptive thoughts.[12]

☑ **Tip: How to deal with anxiety and self-doubt**

It's common to feel nervous before a presentation, important business meeting, or any other activity outside of your comfort zone. However, if you interpret this anxiety as a sign that you're not up to the task, self-doubt will distract you from doing well.[13] What's the remedy?

It turns out that the best way to deal with these situations isn't to fight your nerves (e.g. 'I need to calm down') but instead to reframe anxiety more positively (e.g. 'I'm excited to give this presentation!'). Research shows that people who reframe anxiety as excitement perform better than those who view it as threatening. More precisely, when nerves are viewed positively you adopt an opportunity mindset, which leads to better performance. But when you view nerves negatively, you adopt a threat mindset, which hinders performance.[14]

So next time you're faced with a nerve-wracking situation, don't fight your butterflies; view them as energy and they just might fly in formation.[15]

How to develop self-belief

Self-belief clearly puts you at an advantage when starting a business. People who believe in themselves set ambitious goals, persevere, and are not easily unsettled by stressful situations. But as we learnt earlier, self-belief does not come from nothing. Though confidence is partially genetic,[16,17] there's a tremendous amount you can do to nurture it. And the more you work at developing self-belief the more robust it will be.

Positive self-talk and self-help mantras alone don't work. You need a good mix of experience, encouragement, and education. Let's look at some of the ways you can prepare yourself for entrepreneurship through such a lens.

Experience

The most powerful way to develop self-belief is through experience.[18] Speak to any successful entrepreneur and you will often learn one or both of the following: first, whatever business an entrepreneur is running, it is rarely his or her first attempt at entrepreneurship. Second, whatever industry an entrepreneur is involved in, he or she has more knowledge about it than an outsider does. The following box highlights some examples of this.

 Food for Thought

Richard Reed co-founded *Innocent Drinks* shortly after graduating from university. But the genesis of his entrepreneurial career lay elsewhere. His first venture involved washing windows for neighbours when he was just eight years old. In secondary school, he set up a summer gardening business where he employed friends to work with him. Entrepreneurship wasn't new to Richard. He'd made several attempts at it before.

Another example is Mally Roncal, founder of *Mally Beauty*. While she didn't have the early start in business that Richard Reed had, she had worked in the beauty industry for over a decade. During that time she did make-up for a range of celebrities that included Beyoncé, Rihanna, and Céline Dion. With her experience Mally knew the sector so well that she was confident enough to start a business in the industry.

These are just a few examples of entrepreneurs who leveraged experience to their advantage. You too have a unique set of experiences to draw from. Some may not be entrepreneurial but it's still possible to use them to your advantage. Can you think of any experiences in your life that could be useful in business?

It's worth noting that the experience component of self-belief doesn't have to be grand. It could involve starting a small enterprise while at university, running a side-business while keeping your day job, or working in a sector in which you would like to start a business. But be wary; easy successes will not help you develop a strong sense of self-belief. If success comes without any challenges, you sometimes learn less and may consider yourself just lucky. However, if you pursue ventures that stretch your capabilities and take you out of your comfort zone, you will have a stronger sense of confidence in your ability to overcome future challenges.

Education

Experiences alone aren't enough. Self-belief also requires knowledge and education. This isn't to say you must study business at university or spend hours immersed in textbooks. Instead, the education required for you to have the confidence to succeed in business could involve any of the following:

- Learning from your own experiences
- Studying the success (and failures) of others
- Analysing the market you would like to start a company in
- Speaking to potential customers to understand their needs
- Mastering business fundamentals, some of which you can learn through traditional education (e.g. accounting and finance) and others through practice (e.g. sales, marketing, strategy, and people management)

Such knowledge will help you develop confidence in your ideas and, ultimately, confidence in your ability to succeed.

⌘ Entrepreneur's Insight
Kevin Systrom and Mike Krieger, founders of Instagram

Kevin Systrom, the co-founder of *Instagram*, is a brilliant example of how to use education and knowledge to your advantage. At university, he changed his course from computing to management so he could learn more about business (though with hindsight he admits, 'no undergrad class prepares you to start a start-up – you learn most of it as you do it').[19]

In the years following graduation Kevin joined a marketing team at a small Internet company called *Nextstop*. It was here that Kevin decided to study computer-engineering concepts during evenings and weekends, so he could become a better programmer. It was also during this period that Kevin built an early version of *Instagram*, then called *Burbn* – an app where users could share their location and travel plans.

Along with his co-founder, Mike Krieger, Kevin soon learnt that users were not using *Burbn* as intended. Instead, people were sharing more photos than check-ins. With this knowledge Kevin and Mike scrapped the old idea of location sharing and decided to focus on developing a photo app. With that objective the team studied all the photo apps on the iPhone, identified a clear gap in the market (no photo app at the time offered social features similar to Instagram), and ultimately exploited a fantastic business opportunity.

Encouragement

A final way you can nurture self-belief is through encouragement. This means making time for people who believe in you – people who can offer support in difficult times and cheer you on when things aren't going so well.

Finding encouragement also involves obtaining credible feedback and challenging negative thoughts. And though cultivating self-belief through encouragement is not as powerful as developing confidence through experience and education, a lack of support can be damaging. Believing all the naysayers ('you will never be a success') and not having friends or family to support you only leads to more self-doubt. And if you have already started a business you are more likely to give up if no one is rooting for you. So before you start a venture try to make sure you have sources of encouragement to draw from.

 Food for Thought

In the past, where have you sought or received encouragement from? Did your parents and relatives encourage you during university? Did a friend help you through a particularly difficult time? Encouragement is clearly important whenever we take on challenging tasks but if you are not sure where to find it, the following ideas can help:

- **Role models** – You can find role models in lots of places. If there are none in your social circle, try to explore the autobiographies and stories of people similar to you.

- **Mentors** – Is there anyone in your social circle who you admire? Perhaps someone who's venturesome and more experienced? Ask them out for a coffee to pick their brains on a topic of interest. If you get along, they could make for a great mentor going forward. (Also see *Useful Resources* at the end of the chapter for further guidance.)
- **Other Entrepreneurs** – You can meet and make friends with other entrepreneurs through meet-up groups (try searching Meetup.com for local entrepreneurship groups in your area).

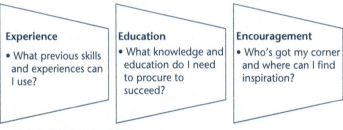

Experience
- What previous skills and experiences can I use?

Education
- What knowledge and education do I need to procure to succeed?

Encouragement
- Who's got my corner and where can I find inspiration?

Figure 3.1: Self-belief checklist

Chapter 3

What comes after self-belief

We have learnt that successful entrepreneurs tap into various forms of experience, education, and encouragement to build their self-belief. But this attribute has limits. For example, confidence alone doesn't always correlate with motivational energy; sometimes the fuel you need to do challenging things comes from elsewhere. The next chapter uncovers this aspect of an entrepreneurial mindset.

Chapter summary

- Self-belief happens when you believe in your ability to succeed. It's the confidence that drives you to action, unlike doubt, which paralyses.
- To do well as an entrepreneur you must first believe in yourself (other people will also find it easier to believe in you when you believe in yourself).

- People who believe in themselves aim high, persevere when things get tough, and are better able to deal with stressful situations.
- The strongest form of self-belief is cultivated through experience and achievement. You can tap into this by gradually taking on challenges in life that stretch your abilities (e.g. starting a side business alongside your job before entering into full-time entrepreneurship).
- Self-belief can also be developed through education, self-directed learning, and encouragement from others.

📖 Reflection

What doubts do you have about starting a successful business? Make a list of these issues and after that, think of ways you could address these doubts. Here are some examples:

- **Doubt:** I've never started a business before...
  - **Resolution:** I can start a small venture by selling vintage items on eBay.
- **Doubt:** I want to start a bakery but don't know if anyone will like my cakes...
  - **Resolution:** I will sell my cakes to friends and family first, to see if people like them.
- **Doubt:** I'm worried my idea will fail and I risk total embarrassment...
  - **Resolution:** What's the worst that could happen if I fail?
  - **Resolution:** Maybe I'm better off starting with a very small investment and if I fail I won't lose much but can learn a lot from it.

Useful resources

- Article: *9 Tips for Finding and Getting the Perfect Mentor* (2015) by Lily Herman
  https://www.themuse.com/advice/9-tips-for-findingand-gettingthe-perfect-mentor

  Why is it worth reading?
  It's a brief summary of the things you can do to get a good mentor. The article also contains links to other bits of advice that are useful, such as how to get someone more experienced to mentor you.

Chapter 4

Passion

What you will gain from this chapter:

1. A more nuanced understanding of passion.
2. An appreciation of the value of passion in business.
3. The ability to identify and cultivate your passions.

Fate works in mysterious ways

When Alicia Keys, Victoria Beckham, and Kim Kardashian were deciding what to wear for their wedding days, they all turned to someone with a peculiar history: the award-winning designer Vera Wang. What makes Vera's story remarkable is that she did not originally plan to start a wedding dress business. From the age of seven Vera wanted to be a figure skater and that's what she spent most of her youth doing.

Over the years Vera's sense of style and fashion stood out to others but it wasn't something she took seriously. Her biggest passion and priority was to compete in the Olympics as a professional figure skater. Unfortunately her hopes were shattered when she failed to qualify for the Olympic team in the 1968 US Figure Skating Championships. And for a while, Vera felt lost.

Unconvinced by the prospects of making it to the Olympics, Vera eventually decided to quit professional skating. But fate wasn't done with her. While working as a window dresser in New York, Vera bumped into an editor of the fashion magazine *Vogue*. After a brief chat the editor was so impressed by Vera's knowledge of fashion that she helped the young student secure a job at the magazine.[1]

Fifteen years later Vera decided to pursue a larger ambition: a promotion to editor-in-chief at *Vogue*. But like the Olympics, Vera's ultimate career goal did not work out. She failed to get the promotion and, as a result, left *Vogue*. Even so, the loss did not cripple or demotivate Vera; it freed her up to explore something else.

When Vera was about to get married, a wardrobe issue presented an opportunity: out of all the wedding dress choices she looked at, nothing excited her so she decided to make a dress for herself. The decision was pivotal. It helped her discover a passion for design and inspired her to start a wedding gown design business at the age of 41.

Vera's story is a glimpse at how passions and careers are never straightforward. We may think that we know where our interests will take us but sometimes new opportunities open us up to passions we never thought we could have.

So what is passion anyway? Why should we care about it in entrepreneurship? Furthermore, how can we discover our passions if we don't yet know what they are? This chapter will help you answer these questions.

 Food for Thought

Did you have any early childhood passions? How did your relationships with them evolve? For example, was there anything you pursued relentlessly only for it to not work out as planned? Perhaps you enrolled for a specific university course but changed direction when your early interests turned out to be different. Or perhaps there was something you weren't originally interested in but when you had some success in it, your interest grew.

Chapter 4

Reflecting on these questions should bring to light the dynamic nature of passion. It changes over time and our capacity to enjoy what we do is more malleable than we realise.

Understanding passion

Every time we read about careers the word *passion* inevitably springs up. We are told that if we follow our passions good things will follow. However, without a clear understanding of passion we may struggle to find what we are passionate about. So what is passion?

The word passion comes from the Latin noun 'passio', which means 'suffering'.[2] Interestingly the Romans translated the term from the ancient Greek word 'paskho', which means 'to put up with' or 'to bear'.[3] This meaning is quite different from the modern use of the word 'passion', which we use to describe a strong enthusiasm for something.[4] But while the English word lacks the nuance of suffering and endurance that the Greek term embodied, 'passion' still relates to emotions that persist. That is, we maintain our interest in passionate activities even when things get tough.

Chapter 4

Key term – Passion:

A genuine interest in something that is personally meaningful and in which you invest considerable time and energy.

Sir Ken Robinson, author of *The Element: How Finding Your Passion Changes Everything*, describes passion as positive spiritual energy. After a long day at work you may be physically drained but if you've worked on things you are passionate about, your 'spiritual' energy (mood, outlook on life, sense of purpose and accomplishment) is higher at the end of the day.

In brief, passion is a genuine interest in something that's personally meaningful and in which you invest significant time and energy.[5] Put another way, passion involves being *interested* and *invested* in something you consider central to your *identity*.

Want to check if you are passionate about something? Figure 4.1 has a few prompts that can help.

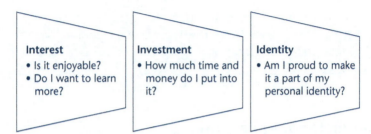

Figure 4.1: A quest for passion

Why passion matters

Starting a business requires sustained effort. For this reason it's advantageous to enter the process with enthusiasm. In a speech at a conference in 2007, the late Steve Jobs put it this way:

> 66 People say you have to have a lot of passion for what you're doing… and it's totally true. And the reason is because it's so hard that if you don't [have passion], any rational person would give up.[6] 99

Let's explore this idea further and look at how passion can help you when starting a business.

Motivational energy

Think back to the most enjoyable thing you've ever worked on. What did it feel like? Now compare that to an activity you did with the least amount of interest or personal meaning. For which of these two activities did you struggle to find motivation and energy?

Passion provides that extra boost of motivation. At its best it makes us forget we are working at all. And at other times we may feel physical exhaustion in the short-term but in the end, passion provides a sense of personal accomplishment that keeps us energised in the long run.

Perseverance

In Chapter 3 we learnt that self-belief – confidence that you have what it takes to succeed – inspires perseverance. But if you face multiple setbacks, confidence may be subdued. In such instances passion can keep you going. This is what drives entrepreneurs to persevere through multiple hurdles. Research shows that entrepreneurs who are passionate about inventing and founding new businesses persist for longer. Their passion and sustained effort helps them overcome obstacles and ultimately contribute to business success.[7]

Influence

Passion is also infectious. If you enjoy what you do you can attract other people to join you with just as much zeal. And, as we will learn later on, you are better off starting a business in a team than you are on your own.

Enthusiasm also helps when you are pitching your idea to potential investors. If you watch an episode of *Dragons' Den* you will notice how a passionate pitch can be more persuasive than a stale one. It isn't surprising then that investors rank passion to be highly important in their investment decisions. However, always be sure to match passion with a well-prepared pitch since no amount of enthusiasm can overcome a poor presentation.[8]

Mental benefits

Finally, studies show that people who engage in activities they are passionate about experience improvements in mood, life satisfaction, and overall happiness.[9] Positive emotions have also been shown to contribute to enhanced creativity and the ability to spot new opportunities. Such benefits are no doubt an asset to the entrepreneurship process.

Chapter 4

☑ Tip: Managing the dark side of passion

Passion has a dark side that's worth a brief mention. When you become so passionate about one thing – your product, business idea, or specific goals – and it becomes the *one* thing in life you cannot live without, you might have a problem.

Research shows that people who can't 'switch-off' from their passions in order to recuperate (e.g. spend time with friends, family, and other interests) risk burning out.[10] Such individuals persist even when it's clear that they shouldn't (e.g. they allow work to be more important than their health).

Accordingly, though starting a business can be all-consuming, remember to switch off from time to time. This will allow you to

> ☑ **Tip: (Continued)**
>
> return to your work feeling more refreshed and energised. Also be sure to maintain enough flexibility to change course if evidence comes to light that you are unlikely to make progress. As we saw in the story of Vera Wang, redirecting your passions can still lead to a fulfilling career and life.

Passion clearly has several benefits in entrepreneurship. But how should we go about discovering what we are passionate about? To answer this question let's take a brief detour through the world of romance before we return to more concrete matters.

Finding your passion

Love at first sight is a rare and remarkable spectacle. An intense passion strikes at the heart even when the couple know little about each other. Yet some of the relationships that come from love at first sight do flourish into the long-term, while others evaporate over a short period. In the latter scenario, one or both parties realise imperfections in one another that conflict with their respective ideas of a perfect partner. And for this reason the couple fail to give another kind of romance a chance.

The other kind of romance burns slower: two people meet but they are not immediately drawn to each other. In fact, they might not even be each other's type. But little by little they get to know each other and start to find qualities that they admire. Still, there may be some imperfections that they have to endure. For some couples this spells the end of the relationship. But for others, the more they learn about each other the more they come to appreciate the good along with the bad, because in their view there's no such thing as a perfect partner.

In some ways finding your passion is a bit like finding love. Some people believe in the search for a perfect *fit*, much like love at first sight, while others believe in a more open approach, where there's no one 'perfect match' but many opportunities that could *develop* into a good fit. Psychologists have a term for these two perspectives: 'fit theory' and 'develop theory'. Both approaches can lead to successful outcomes but their suitability, as we will see below, depends on personal circumstance.[11]

Fit theory

The fit theory of passion is what we tend to read about the most. It's also the view that most people subscribe to. In brief, fit theory advocates argue that you should seek out things that you enjoy from the outset – a love-at-first-sight kind of passion. This view of passion is wonderful if you are lucky enough to find what you love.

 Food for Thought

A lucky few discover their passions early. When entrepreneur Emily Cummins was just four years old her grandfather gave her a hammer and taught her how to make things from spare parts. She was hooked immediately. The event sparked Emily's passion for sustainable design and right away she knew that was her calling.[12] From then on Emily continued to nurture her love for invention and has since gone on to win a range of awards that include *Young Entrepreneur of the Year* and *Barclays Woman of the Year*.

Like Emily, you may have interests that captivated you right away. Can you think of some examples? If so, did your enjoyment of the activity thrive or did it wane over time? What other pursuits took your fancy from the get-go? These will all be examples of fit theory passions.

Develop theory

For those of us who have been searching for years and just can't figure out what we are passionate about, develop theory gives us hope. In this view passion can be developed in almost any activity, as long as there's some initial interest, mastery of skill, and success. This view of passion is a less popular approach but stories of it are more prevalent than we think. An example is provided in the next *Entrepreneur's Insight*.

Chapter 4

⌘ Entrepreneur's Insight
Felix Dennis, founder of Felix Publishing

Before Lord Alan Sugar was chosen by the BBC to host *The Apprentice*, the TV channel had failed to recruit someone else for the job: the late entrepreneur and poet Felix Dennis. Though he's remembered for his eccentricity and generosity (he left £400m of his fortune to a forest preservation charity), Felix did not always show much interest in magazines (an industry he'd make millions from).

In his teens Felix wanted to be a musician. He was confident in his song-writing abilities and enjoyed promoting and marketing his band, *The Flamingos*. It wasn't until many years later when he reluctantly had to flog magazines for extra cash that he realised something: with the right sales technique, he could make a lot of money from selling magazines.

Felix went on to develop his tactics, and as he got better at selling and marketing he started to make more cash and grew more confident. Bear in mind that up until this point Felix wasn't pursuing some predefined passion. He was just looking for ways to make a quick buck. Regardless, he was also developing skills that would prove useful when another opportunity arose.

That opportunity came when Felix noticed the growing popularity of the martial artist Bruce Lee. And though Felix did not have a passion for kung fu – he had only watched ten minutes of Bruce Lee's movie *Enter the Dragon* – he saw how excited people were about the genre and decided to create a magazine around it. Fortunately the venture paid off handsomely and catapulted Felix's career as a magazine publisher.[13]

Was Felix born with a passion for publishing? No. His first love was music. But after he became good at selling magazines Felix developed a passion for the industry and built an amazing company as a result.

Passion in entrepreneurship

Earlier in the chapter we met Emily Cummins, who discovered her passion for invention at the age of four. When your passion is this obvious you can immediately start to explore ways of incorporating it in your entrepreneurial journey. Indeed, your current passions can be a great starting point to find a business idea if you don't already have one. And as long as your business is based on something you are genuinely interested in, you will be more energised and more likely to succeed.

If you don't know what your passion is you can adopt the develop theory of passion. This is because it's possible to cultivate passion in lots of other areas, even if you may not enjoy them at first.[14]

Felix Dennis, who we met in a previous *Entrepreneur's Insight*, did not spend years searching for a 'perfect-fit' passion to base his business on. Instead, he channelled the skills he had (sales and marketing) to something people wanted. This just so happened to be a magazine that would cash in on a growing trend. According to his own account, Felix became an entrepreneur by accident.[15] He secured a fulfilling career not by searching for the *one* thing he was passionate about, but through the application of skill in order to profit from an emerging opportunity. This enabled Felix to build a publishing empire that produced successful titles such as *Men's Fitness*, *Auto Express*, and *The Week*.

In sum, while it's wise to be entrepreneurial in something you're passionate about, don't be disheartened if you haven't figured out what your passions are. Instead, take stock of your skills and look for areas where you can apply them masterfully and for the benefit of other people.

Chapter 4

> ☑ **Tip: How to find your passion in entrepreneurship**
>
> Felix Dennis had some words of advice for those of us who are yet to discover our passions. The following themes, adapted from the publishing mogul's thoughts, summarise his guidance.[16]
>
> 1. **Inclinations** – What things do you naturally gravitate towards? What interests you the most? If you are passionate about medieval art, for example, there might not be an obvious business concept to build around it. But is there anything linked to it that other people would find valuable?
> 2. **Aptitude** – What skills come easily to you? For Felix it was sales, marketing, and writing. For Emily Cummins it was design and invention. For Vera Wang it was a sense of style. What are the things your friends say you are good at? What are you naturally gifted at? Have you received exceptional recognition (awards, high grades, money) for a particular activity? You may be able to commercialise these skills if you can apply them to a promising business area.

☑ **Tip: (Continued)**

3. **Luck** – Are there any lucky events you can take advantage of? Felix got his break when he saw a massive queue of fans lining up at a cinema in Leicester Square for a Bruce Lee movie. It was then that he decided to create a magazine for fans of kung fu. What emerging opportunities can you apply your aptitudes and inclinations to? If you find success with these opportunities, you may find yourself becoming more passionate about them.

The long road ahead

The great thing about starting your own business is that you get to decide what you want to work on. If you are passionate about music you can reinvent the record label business. If you're passionate about travel you can create a travel media publishing business. And if you're not sure what your passions are, you can experiment with areas that pique your interest until you find something worth pursuing. But when you do find or develop that passion, be ready for the long road ahead. Passion will help you work harder and more creatively but you will also need strategies to help you endure the long road ahead. The next chapter deals with this aspect of the entrepreneurial mindset.

⌘ **Entrepreneur's Insight**
Julien Callede, co-founder of Made.com

Work hard and put some fun into it. If you don't put some fun into it you won't be able to work hard for long. So you need to be excited about what you do, either because you believe in the product you sell or because there is fun in your job on a day-to-day basis. Enjoying it [and] believing [in what you sell] is important because you can do anything short-term – a month, a year, or two years – but we've been running for four years and a half. Working together has been great. We love it. [But] if all of us didn't believe very deeply in what we are selling, that would have been hell.

Chapter summary

- Passion is a genuine interest in something that's personally meaningful and in which you invest time and energy.
- If you have passion you can work longer, harder, and smarter.
- If you already know what your passions are, think of ways you can include them in your business ideas.
- If you don't know what your passions are, don't worry. Research shows that you can cultivate a passion in almost anything.
- Sometimes passion only comes after you've had some success in an area. So keep an open mind, experiment, and be prepared to take advantage of any lucky breaks you may get.

 Reflection

Can't figure out what you're passionate about? Use the questions below to help you generate some ideas:

- **Inclinations**
  - What do you enjoy doing?
  - Where do you spend most of your free time (and money)?
  - What kind of work would you do if money weren't a problem?
- **Talents**
  - What have you always been naturally good at?
  - Are there any skills you've picked up quicker than other people?
  - What comes easily to you?
- **Opportunities**
  - Have you had any lucky breaks? Do you have any contacts in a particularly attractive industry that you can call on for help?
  - Are there trends or emerging opportunities where you could apply your inclinations and talents?

If you have many passions and can't figure out which ones to focus on, use the questions below to help you generate some ideas:

- **Interests**
  - Which passion do you enjoy the most?

- **Investment**
  - Which passion do you spend the most time (or money) on?
- **Identity**
  - Which passion would you most proudly identify with?

Useful resources

- Book: *So Good They Can't Ignore You* (2012) by Cal Newport

  Why is it worth reading?
  This book's advice is provocative. 'Don't follow your passion,' it argues. But after reading it you will come to appreciate that there is another path to career success. You don't always have to follow passions you are born with; you can develop new passions and be just as successful!

Endurance

What you will gain from this chapter:

1. Appreciate the value of persevering in business.
2. Learn how to prepare for the challenges ahead.
3. Be able to deal with setbacks effectively.
4. Know when to quit if things don't work out.

Obstacles are mandatory

No matter how well you prepare when starting a business, there will be obstacles. Competition could turn fierce; you may need more money than you'd planned for; a co-founder may abandon your venture; or a personal emergency could bring your business to a complete standstill.

In light of these circumstances it's prudent to come to terms with the fact that when you enter the arena of entrepreneurship you will not leave unscathed. Entrepreneurship is inherently uncertain and things don't always work out as planned. However, if you can endure – that is, sustain your efforts in the face of obstacles – you will be more likely to create a successful business. What's more, there are steps you can take to improve your ability to endure. This chapter will provide such guidance. It will also help you identify when it's time to throw in the towel because as it turns out, persevering endlessly has a downside. But before we get to that let's briefly review why endurance is key to being an effective entrepreneur.

⌘ Entrepreneur's Insight
James Dyson, founder of Dyson

Stories of entrepreneurs who've overcome the most difficult of challenges are plentiful. Take James Dyson for example, inventor of the famous Dyson vacuum cleaners. In his autobiography, aptly titled *Against the Odds*, Dyson recalls how in building his company he struggled with debt, expensive legal battles, and several rejections from manufacturers. But only after years of persevering – along with 5,127 attempts at developing a bagless vacuum cleaner – did he emerge with a prosperous business.

⌘ Entrepreneur's Insight
Angie Hicks, founder of Angie's List

Angie Hicks, a technology entrepreneur, also struggled in her early days of setting up a business. She spent months doing door-to-door sales in an attempt to sign up customers and would often cry from frustration.

Like many before her, Angie thought about giving up on more than one occasion. While her friends were being hired at prestigious companies Angie was having doors slammed in her face. But she endured. And thanks to her perseverance Angie now runs a successful business that employs more than 1,000 people.[1]

The value of endurance

Success is not linear

It's important to endure and persevere in business because success is not linear. Nassim Taleb, an ex-hedge fund manager who studies and writes about probabilities, offers the following analogy.[2]

When we are studying a subject we like to think that for each hour of effort that we put in we will get an hour's worth of returns. Thinking about success this way is intuitive: the more you do, the more you get, just like the graph to the left in Figure 5.1. But think back to a time when you had to study something hard. Did you understand it immediately? Or, did you have to ruminate on it for days before everything made sense?

> **Key term – Endurance:**
> The ability to sustain efforts in the face of unpleasant or difficult situations.

More often than not, insights in your studies follow the latter process. To the outside world your triumph looks like overnight success (the 'eureka' moment) when in fact you've been chipping away at a problem or concept for several days (see graph to the right in Figure 5.1).

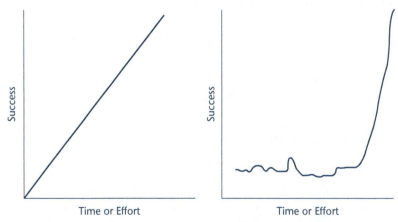

Figure 5.1: What we think success looks like (left graph) vs. what success really looks like (right graph)

Entrepreneurship is similar to the study analogy. You may have to work for a long time on one or more ventures before things really take off. But if you give up early, perhaps at the first sign of trouble, you may never get to the reward.

☑ **Tip: How long should you persevere for?**

Dave McClure is an investor with hundreds of businesses in his portfolio. In his view a great company can take anywhere from five to ten years to build. But he also believes that you can usually tell whether a company's product (or service) is 'at least good' within 6–12 months.[3]

In light of these timelines, if you have a business idea you believe in, be prepared to endure with the business for at least 6–12 months. This way you will have enough time and feedback to gauge whether the business is worth pursuing in the long-term.

Acute learning opportunities

Another reason why endurance matters in entrepreneurship is the personal growth it can stimulate. The longer you persevere, the more opportunities you get to learn from challenges, and the more you can grow into a more effective entrepreneur. Moreover, challenges and setbacks are better teachers than success. This is because when something doesn't work out it makes a greater impression on you than the euphoria of success. In short, hard lessons are hard to forget.

Now that we are more familiar with the benefits of enduring, how can we do so productively? The following sections will show you how.

Preparing for obstacles

Write a pre-mortem

Facing a challenge you expect is easier than being caught off guard. In fact, you can avoid many pitfalls if you anticipate them. One way of achieving this is by performing a pre-mortem before you start a venture. In medicine, a post-mortem is an exercise that can identify the cause of death after the fact. In business, a pre-mortem is the opposite.[4] Here's how it works.

Before starting your business, assume it has failed. Then make a list of what could have gone wrong. Here are some examples of possible causes of failure.

- We ran out of money too soon, since costs were higher than expected.
- A competitor emerged and copied our product.
- Customers did not respond well to our marketing and we lost sales.
- We fell out with a co-founder.

After that, pick out the top risks and make a plan for how you will mitigate them. Here are some examples.

- Risk of running out of money too soon – mitigate by securing extra funding before starting the business.
- Risk of competitors copying our product – make sure we have a defendable unique selling point that's not easy to copy.
- Risk of falling out with a co-founder – have a plan of action for when disagreements happen between co-founders.

Pre-mortems may sound grim but imagining that your business has failed is a more powerful way of identifying risks than overconfident planning. Once you know what the potential challenges are, not only are you less likely to be unsettled by them when they arrive, you will also be better prepared to overcome them.

Chapter 5

 Food for Thought

Do you have any goals to which you can apply the pre-mortem concept? It may be a presentation you are due to give at your workplace. It could be a job interview. It could even simply be a personal goal to get in shape. Whatever the aim, take a few minutes to apply a pre-mortem. You will be better prepared and more able to overcome challenges this way.

Get comfortable being uncomfortable

Another method of preparing for the challenges ahead, some of which will demand that you act decisively under pressure, is to get out of your comfort zone more often. You can achieve this by 'practising' under mild levels of stress. This is because research shows that rehearsing under pressure trains you to deal with high-stake situations more effectively.[5] Consider the process a vaccine of sorts: low-stake situations that take you out of your comfort zone are like a weak form of a virus that helps you become immune to future attacks.[6]

At university, examples of such preparation would have included doing mock exams under timed conditions or rehearsing for job interviews with a friend. But in entrepreneurship you could, for example, present your business idea to a friend and ask them to play devil's advocate. This way they can help you practise how to respond to critics of your concept.

In sum, if you become comfortable with the uncomfortable you will be able to think and work more clearly when things get tough.

How to persevere

To persevere in business you need to develop habits that weaken the impact of an obstacle or a setback. Every individual will have their unique style on how to deal with rough patches in entrepreneurship but if you can adopt some of the behaviours below you will be able to persevere.

Have a bias for optimism

Great comebacks thrive on optimism. Not only that but some of the greatest stories of endurance are always based on hope. One such story is that of Sir Ernest Shackleton's historic voyage to the Antarctic. When the expedition turned sour, his crew put on a brave face despite slim chances of survival. And though the crew did have doubts it was more effective for them to have hope and strive for survival than to expect failure, which would have been a premature admission of defeat.

When you start your business and things don't go as planned, you too should have a bias for hope over pessimism. This helps you to focus on finding solutions to problems rather than fretting over the hurdles you face.

But what if something knocks you back significantly? What if, for example, you pitch your product or service to an important person but they turn you down? Again, a bias for optimism helps and you can even do more by adjusting your interpretation of events. Here's how.

According to research pioneered by psychologist Dr Martin Seligman, pessimists view negative situations differently from how optimists view them. Pessimists see bad events as:

- Personal – e.g. 'She won't buy my product because she doesn't like me.'
- Permanent – e.g. 'My first product didn't do well so I'll never come up with any good product ideas.'
- Pervasive – e.g. 'Since I'm not a good sales person I'll never be good at entrepreneurship or anything else in life!'

These interpretations make people feel helpless and anxious. In contrast, an optimistic entrepreneur would view challenges as:

- Impersonal – 'She didn't buy my product because her needs were different.'
- Temporary – 'My idea failed, but I'll come up with something better.'
- Confined – 'My sales skills need work, but I'll make up for it with excellent marketing.'

Studies show that people who interpret negative events in a more positive light benefit in several ways. They are more effective at solving problems; they are less prone to depression; and they recover from setbacks faster than pessimists do.[7] So next time something doesn't go according to plan be sure to interpret it as being impersonal, temporary, and confined.

> ☑ **Tip: How to respond to a setback**
>
> Being optimistic is not just about sugar coating what happens to you. It's about assessing events accurately and positively. One way of achieving this is by taking care to note any inaccuracies in your thinking, particularly extreme positions that involve phrases like:
>
> - 'I _always_ mess up.'
> - 'This will _never_ work.'
> - '_Everything_ in my life is going to fall apart because of this.'

> ### ☑ Tip: (Continued)
>
> You are better off replacing such extreme positions with something realistic but optimistic. Table 5.1 shows how a positive-minded entrepreneur might respond to a poor customer product review, for example:
>
> **Table 5.1:** A positive take on negative reviews
>
> | Don't Take Things Personally | Don't Expect Things to Be Permanent | Don't Make Things Pervasive or Bigger Than They Are |
> |---|---|---|
> | Businesses get bad reviews all the time. It's never personal and it's simply about a customer not having their needs met. It says nothing about me as a human being. | One bad review doesn't mean there's more to follow. As long as I remedy any issues now, this won't last forever. We will get positive reviews in time. | One bad review doesn't mean we have a fundamentally bad business. Look at all the other positive feedback we've had. It's impossible to please everyone. Let's focus on doing the best we can. |

Remember the 'why'

Reminding yourself why you started something can energise you to overcome difficulties during your venture. For instance, if you started a business to solve an important problem, reminding yourself how your venture will impact the lives of people could motivate you to persevere. On the other hand, if you started a business with the hopes of making a lot of money, reminding yourself what that money will do for you can also be motivating.

A word of caution, however: starting a business just because you want to make a lot of money is a terrible reason when used on its own. For one, people who do it just for the money are less likely to endure early business losses (most ventures lose money in the first few months). Second, entrepreneurs whose business is not solving a problem they care deeply about often throw in the towel when the prospects of making money aren't immediate. But if your reasons are genuine and deeply meaningful (remember the chapter on passion!) you will be more likely to persevere.

Don't stand still; take action

Business is dynamic and entrepreneurs who stand still for too long can be out of the game before they know it. To avoid this fate, have a bias for action whenever you come across an obstacle. If something seems intimidating, break it into smaller components so that it's more manageable. This also makes progress more visible and if it's clear that you are moving forward (no matter how small the steps are) you will be motivated to persevere. As the Chinese proverb says, 'to get through the hardest journey we need take only one step at a time, but we must keep on stepping'.

☑ **Tip: Problem-solving toolkit**

Obstacle Example: *I'd like to have my product featured on a range of blogs. But all the bloggers I've emailed won't respond to my messages.*

(1) Think Broadly: Negative events narrow our thinking. But to solve problems effectively you have to first open your mind to broader possibilities, even those you wouldn't normally consider. Thinking 'outside the box' may sound like a cliché but make it a habit whenever you come across a challenge. You may find more creative solutions this way.

Action Example: Email might not be the most impressive method to make first contact. Maybe I can find a list of blogger events and meet key bloggers in person.

(2) Re-word the Problem: You can also inspire creative solutions by restating or redefining a problem. This involves rewording the issue and digging into it as much as you can to identify the root cause. Asking lots of 'whys' is usually a good start.

Action Example: Why aren't bloggers responding to my emails? Is it because I have a boring product? Is it because popular bloggers get tons of emails from people like me? If it's the latter then maybe I need to find another point of contact that's less crowded.

(3) Adjust Your Goal: If a problem seems intractable it might be time to set your sails for more favourable winds.

Action Example: I'm not getting anywhere with bloggers so I won't pursue them. Instead, I will reach out to hosts of popular podcasts that discuss topics related to my product or service.

Cultivate a healthy social network

Being an entrepreneur can get lonely quickly because it's a minority occupation. If you start a business you will probably be the only entrepreneur amongst your friends. Even so, you shouldn't let your relationships wane. A great amount of research shows that social capital – your network of friends, family, and mentors – can have an impact on how well you can withstand stress. It also contributes to your mental and physical well-being.[8]

This advice seems obvious, since it is our friends and family who support us in times of need. Yet you would be surprised how many entrepreneurs forget the importance of a healthy social network. So before and after you start your business, remember the saying, 'dig your well before you're thirsty'. That is, always keep your relationships healthy. You never know when they will have to come to your rescue.

When to quit

Admittedly there are some obstacles no amount of endurance or perseverance can overcome. *Homejoy*, an online platform that connected customers to cleaners, was once a poster child for on-demand services. Yet despite raising over £20 million from top investors and expanding to over 30 cities, the forces working against it were too great to bear. The business eventually ran out of money and had to close shop, no thanks to stiff competition, customer service issues, and a number of lawsuits.

Sometimes your hand will be forced and you will have to walk away. And on other occasions it may not be so much of an outside force you can't control but rather an inner debate you have to resolve yourself. So how can you decide when it's time to quit? Marketing expert and entrepreneur Seth Godin offers the following advice in his book, *The Dip*.

First, before you embark on a new venture it's worth taking the time to articulate what factors will help you decide whether to quit or not. Without a pre-meditated set of aims that will tell you whether the business is working or not, you may end up in limbo and have no idea whether to keep persisting or whether to try something else. But if you know in advance the factors that would cause you to quit, it can help you with that decision later on.

Second, if it becomes clear that no one really needs your product, then switch lanes as fast as you can before wasting any more effort. In addition to that, if after significant efforts you still make no progress then by definition your venture will either be standing still or falling behind. In either of these cases, the idea isn't worth pursuing.

Finally, if your 'why' for starting a venture wanes and you develop an acute dispassion for the business, then it's time to quit. If you don't see any long-term potential or you realise that a venture's future prospects aren't compelling enough, then quit.

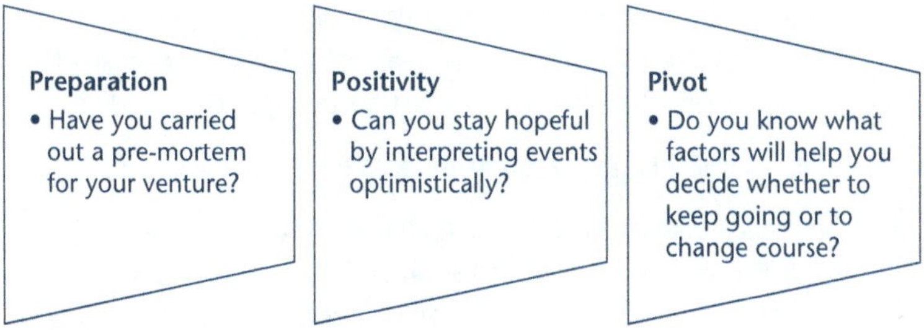

Preparation
- Have you carried out a pre-mortem for your venture?

Positivity
- Can you stay hopeful by interpreting events optimistically?

Pivot
- Do you know what factors will help you decide whether to keep going or to change course?

Figure 5.2: What it takes to endure

⌘ Entrepreneur's Insight
Xavier Helgesen, CEO and co-founder of Off Grid Electric

Not sure when to persevere or when to quit? Here's a unique perspective on the matter:

I think you can never completely know. I'm sure there are some times when people would have told us to drop what we were doing. So you know, I think the best thing you can ask yourself is, how many people would be really disappointed if you went away, and not just the people already using your product but the people who might like to use your product? If there are a lot of people who would be incredibly disappointed if you didn't exist then you're probably on the right track.

Food for Thought

What's your motivation for starting a business? Do you think it's compelling enough to help you endure the challenges ahead? Here are two common types of motivation that inspire people to start businesses. An example is provided in each case but see if there is anything you can relate to.

(1) Push Motivation: starting a business out of necessity

- After learning that her daughter was being bullied at school, Julie Deane, founder of the *Cambridge Satchel Company*, took up entrepreneurship so she could afford to find a better school for her child. She was motivated out of a necessity to provide a good education for her daughter.

(2) Pull Motivation: starting a business to fulfil a personal desire

- *Apple* co-founder Steve Jobs wanted to build a great company that would outlast him. And though he was partially motivated by money, he was more driven by a desire to contribute something imaginative to the world. He wanted to create something as rich and as expressive as the works of artists that he admired.[9]

Chapter 5

More than effort

Endurance is synonymous with stamina. We sustain efforts in the face of resistance, hoping that our tenacity will pay off. Indeed, the process is a disciplined kind of effort that can beat talent when talent doesn't work hard. But entrepreneurship isn't just about slogging away and doing the same thing over and over again. We must also adopt a mindset that's willing to abandon the status quo in favour of more creative approaches. The next chapter will expand on this aspect of an entrepreneurial mindset.

Chapter summary

- Endurance – the ability to sustain efforts when you are faced with challenges – is critical to entrepreneurship.
- Without persevering you may never get to the rewards that await those who work harder and for longer.

- To endure the challenges ahead, be sure to prepare and anticipate risks by using the pre-mortem exercise.
- In difficult times favour optimism over pessimism, for it enables you to focus on solutions to problems rather than allowing you to become distracted by negative thoughts.
- If after a reasonable amount of time you don't make progress, consider moving on to a different venture. But only do this if you have exhausted all reasonable means of achieving your goals.

 Reflection

This chapter has offered guidance on how to persevere. Feel free to return here whenever you feel you need a few ideas on how to persist. But before starting your business try the following exercise to reinforce some of the ideas we've discussed.

Preparation

What are the things that may cause your venture to fail? How can you mitigate these risks? Feel free to jot down some ideas on these issues.

Positivity

Is there a past negative event you can apply some positivity to in order to appreciate the benefits of optimism? For example, one could interpret a poor exam result as follows:

- Impersonal – *A bad exam result doesn't reflect on my worth as a human being.*
- Impermanent – *Not doing well on an exam isn't something that will have a permanent effect since I can always take the exam again.*
- Isolated – *Performing poorly here doesn't mean the rest of my life is doomed.*

Pivot

- Is there anything that would make you quit a particular venture? Identify these factors early on so that if they happen, you know when to quit.

Chapter 5

Useful resources

- Book: *Endurance: Shackleton's Incredible Voyage* (2014) by Alfred Lansing

  Why is it worth reading?
  This book is a true account of a survival story that involved a voyage across the Antarctic seas. Shackleton and his crew of 27 men made it back alive but only after enduring the worst of mother nature. If you want to learn about perseverance, leadership, and camaraderie, this 400-pager is a must-read.

- Movie: *The Revenant* (2015) starring Leonardo DiCaprio and Tom Hardy

  Why is it worth watching?
  If you don't have time to read *Endurance*, watch this movie. It's an Oscar-winning film set in the 1820s and follows a frontiersman on a survival journey that's a testament to the resilience of the human spirit.

- Movie: *Pursuit of Happyness* (2006) starring Will Smith

  Why is it worth watching?
  This is one of Will Smith's best movies. Based on the life of the stockbroker and entrepreneur Chris Gardner, the movie shows that no matter how bad things get, hope and hard work can transform your life.

Creativity

What you will gain from this chapter:

1. Learn what creativity is.
2. Know what creativity looks like in entrepreneurship.
3. Be able to nurture and boost your creativity.

Wine and books

It's hard to believe that a 15th century wine press – a device used to crush grapes – is part of the reason why you're able to read this book. But as strange as it may seem, there is a connection. In the 1400s, after a failed business venture, entrepreneur Johannes Gutenberg decided to explore the technology wine merchants used in their businesses. Gutenberg's previous venture involved manufacturing 'magical' mirrors for religious people, so alcohol was quite the deviation. Still, it wasn't wine he was interested in; Gutenberg had other motives.[1]

For more than 4,000 years books were produced and copied by hand. The process was painstaking. One book alone could take more than a year to produce and only the rich could afford to buy one. Gutenberg saw this as an opportunity. The reason why he was so interested in winemaking machines was because he realised that he could borrow their technology for a new venture. Gutenberg's creative insight was that the screw mechanisms used to crush grapes could also be adapted for use in the printing process. This way, people wouldn't have to press ink to paper by hand.[2] Though the connection seems obvious now, the link that Gutenberg made was imaginative. He took something that was used to make alcohol and used it to create one of man's greatest inventions – the printing press.

Gutenberg's story is just one example of a creative entrepreneur. There are many more stories of creativity in entrepreneurship that range from clever marketing schemes to new products and services. Creativity lies at the heart of what entrepreneurship is and without it you would not be able to build a compelling business.

In this chapter, we'll look at what creativity is, the conditions under which it thrives, the tools you can employ to be more creative, and the process you can go through to facilitate your inventiveness.

What is creativity?

The ancient Greek scientist Archimedes is tasked by his King to investigate if a particular crown is made of pure gold or whether it's a fake. For a while the scientist thinks hard about the problem but eventually relents and decides to relax with a bath. As he slides into the bathtub, the water overflows and spills to the side. Archimedes gets a light bulb moment: he realises he can calculate the volume of the crown by measuring the amount of water it displaces, just like his body dispersed the water in the bath. The volume can then be used to measure the crown's density and ultimately whether it's made of pure gold. After the discovery Archimedes leaps out of his bath, runs into the streets naked, and shouts 'eureka!' The insight is unexpected and ingenious. It's creative.

Joy Mangano hardly fits the stereotype of an inventor: she's not an engineer or a scientist. Joy studied business administration at a relatively unknown university. She was a single mother of three and worked as a waitress for extra cash. She also did a lot of cleaning at home but hated getting her hands dirty when squeezing water out of her mop. She began to wonder if it was possible to make a mop that could be rinsed without getting her hands wet. Joy reviewed various types of mops to see what performed best and after working through several combinations of ideas, she designed the 'Miracle Mop' – a mop that you can wring out by twisting its interlocking handles; all without getting your hands wet.[3] Joy went on to make millions by reinventing an ordinary item and her story inspired a movie starring Jennifer Lawrence. Joy's idea is fresh, imaginative, and most certainly creative.

In light of the above, what is creativity? Creativity is a process of coming up with new ideas that are useful. Notice, however, that there are two requirements. First, the idea should be new in some way (a complete copy of something else doesn't count). Second, the idea must be useful (speaking gibberish might be original but it's useless and therefore cannot be considered creative). In entrepreneurship, creativity takes the same definition. It's the process of coming up with new ideas that can generate value.

Creativity in entrepreneurship

When you start a business, creativity can spark brilliant marketing campaigns, it can help you sell your ideas better, and it can also help you generate novel solutions to a range of business problems.

> **Key term – Creativity:**
> The process of generating new, useful, ideas.

For instance, decades ago a business in New York received complaints that the lifts in its building were too slow. When tenants threatened to leave, the owners of the building did not simply throw money at expensive engineering to make the lifts go faster. Instead, they gave the problem some thought and arrived at a novel solution: install mirrors in the lobby and lifts. It turned out that people were willing to tolerate longer waiting times if they were preoccupied with something else. Indeed, the mirrors proved to be a useful distraction, with some people using them to freshen up before their meetings.[4] Today, lobby and lift mirrors are commonplace,[5] but who knew that such a simple solution could be so effective.

Creativity is definitely a tool worth using in entrepreneurship. It's a skill you should take every opportunity to employ because it can help you save money and attract more customers. Thankfully, decades of research suggest that it is possible to become more creative[6] and in the following sections we will explore how you can do just that.

Nurturing creativity

Creativity requires fertile grounds to flourish. The foundation of this fertility involves a number of factors that can increase your ability to be creative. Let's consider each of these factors in turn.

Genuine interest

You are more likely to come up with creative ideas when you are genuinely interested in an activity. In studies of geniuses, accomplished scientists, artists, as well as the general population, we find that creativity thrives when there's enjoyment, satisfaction of curiosity, and personal meaning in the work being done.[7] On the other hand, if you are mainly driven by external rewards (money, accolades, recognition) you are more likely to look for shortcuts. In such cases people do just enough to get a reward and usually don't spend as much time exploring more unconventional ideas.

Non-judgement

Fear of failure kills creativity. When all you're concerned about is making sure that you never come up with bad ideas, your ability to generate novel concepts diminishes. So it's important to hold back judgement in the early stages of creativity (we'll come back to this later). Also, don't worry about what other people make of your early ideas. The president of *Pixar*, the film studio responsible for the hit movie franchise *Toy Story*, puts it this way: you are not your idea! If your identity is too attached to your ideas it's easy to be offended when other people challenge them.[8] So kill the ego if you want to create freely.

Knowledge

There's a saying: you need to learn the rules before you can break them. Highly creative people learn a subject well before they can generate fresh ideas. Indeed, the accomplished creative usually takes this to the extreme. For instance Mozart, who already had a work ethic of an adult in his childhood,[9] once remarked:

> 66 It is a mistake to think that the practise of my art has become easy to me. I assure you, dear friend, no one has given so much care to the

study of composition as I. There is scarcely a famous master in music whose works I have not frequently and diligently studied. 🔊🔊

Mozart studied his craft for more than 10,000 hours in his life but this isn't something you need to do if you want to be creative in business. You just need to invest some time in learning more about a particular subject before you can craft imaginative insights.

☑ **Tip: In Practice**

To build creative knowledge:

- Read lots of books, magazines, and websites on a topic.
- Study successful businesses and entrepreneurs.
- Find a mentor or expert to learn from.

Anti-knowledge

Paradoxically, too much knowledge and experience can limit creative breakthroughs. For example, the electronics giant *Sony* initially abandoned their research on music CDs in the 1970s. They believed that it wasn't worth developing a CD that could hold 18 hours of music. In their view, no one would buy such a disc, especially since a 300-song CD would be priced at £100 or more. Where did Sony get these estimates? In the '70s, *Sony* thought that a CD would have to be the same size as a previous invention – the vinyl. Back then, vinyl discs were 30 cm in diameter and *Sony* assumed that CDs would also need to be just as big.[10] Of course this turned out to be a poor assumption and was quickly rectified.

The lesson here is this: when you allow your thinking to be constrained by what has come before, you limit your creative potential. So be prepared to throw out conventions if you want to be more imaginative.

Quantity

Creative individuals are known for a limited number of great works. What we overlook, however, is that extraordinary ideas require a prolific work ethic. For example, the entrepreneur Thomas Edison had more than 1,000 inventions to his name (many were useless). The Beatles recorded more than 200 songs (out of this figure less than

10 percent were number ones). And Picasso produced more than 10,000 paintings (only a few hundred are well known). It's important to appreciate that if you want to come up with something novel you may have to go through lots and lots of ideas.

In short, creativity is often a numbers game.[11] In fact, research in the area tells us that a high quantity of ideas yields higher creative output.[12] People who come up with lots of ideas get more chances to learn from their mistakes[13] and end up exploring more unconventional paths. On the other hand, if you are too judgemental and worry about coming up with the perfect idea right away you may not create anything of impact.

Divergent thinking

Before describing divergent thinking, it's worth considering its opposite: convergent thinking. You use convergent thinking all the time. It's when you use the analytical part of your brain to hone in on one correct answer. This type of thinking works great in exams since there's usually only one solution. However, convergent thinking is less helpful when it comes to generating ideas. You are better off using divergent thinking, which is a more open way of exploring ideas. Divergent thinking does not hone in on one answer. Instead, it allows for a multitude of perspectives and possible solutions. So when you get your creative hat on, be open to possibilities that seem unrelated and always aim to look beyond the most obvious solutions.

> ☑ **Tip: Brainstorm**
>
> If you're trying to come up with an idea, start off by brainstorming more options than you need. If you would normally feel comfortable coming up with ten ideas, try 30 or more instead. This will stretch your imagination and lead to some very unusual insights. Be sure not to repeat yourself, however, and only come up with unique concepts on each branch.

How to generate creative ideas

Now that we know what type of conditions inspire creativity, what mechanisms can you use to generate creative ideas? There are several methods but below we will look at three that are effective.

Shuffle concepts

Nothing is truly original. All creative ideas are inspired in part by what came before. Take the immensely popular *Twilight* novels, for example. The books' author Stephenie Meyer was inspired by ideas from classics such as *Wuthering Heights* and *Romeo and Juliet*. Or take *Boohoo.com* for instance. It's no surprise that some people refer to it as an 'online *Primark*', especially since the business combines discount fashion (maxi dresses for as low as £5!) with online retail.

To generate new ideas, try combining unusual or opposing concepts together.[14] Something special happens when you get this right – you can create an entirely new category of products or services that are memorable. Here are a few examples:

- Non-alcoholic beer
- Affordable luxury
- Ice cream burger
- Silent disco

 Food for Thought

Michael Jackson did not invent the moonwalk; he commercialised it. *Apple* did not invent online music distribution; they refined it. And *Google* did not invent web search; they perfected it. Instead of trying to create something that's 100 percent original, are there any current ideas you could reinvent in your own unique way?

Stretch concepts

You can generate new ideas by stretching known concepts to new applications.[15] At the beginning of this chapter we learnt that Gutenberg invented the printing press by using screw mechanisms from a wine press. He stretched an already established idea in order to apply it to a new domain. This is what stretching concepts involves and if you are short on ideas, it's one of the ways you can boost your creativity.

☑ **Tip: In Practice**

Here are some examples of activities that stretch concepts:

- Turning a spare bedroom into a mini B&B (the company *Airbnb.com* facilitates this)
- Using a hair dryer to defog a bathroom mirror
- Using shaving cream to remove rug stains
- Books as a doorstop? (hopefully not this one!)

Scan for catalysts

How about if you have no concepts to combine or expand? In this instance you should seek a catalyst: a small idea to build upon. As we discovered in the myths of entrepreneurship, no great idea ever arrives fully formed. Very few business ideas ever start that way. So don't put pressure on yourself to come up with something ingenious. Instead, 'scratch' around for small bits of inspiration and concepts you can build on. The acclaimed choreographer Twyla Tharp describes the process in her book *The Creative Habit* as something akin to scratching a lottery ticket. You may not be sure what will emerge but if you keep scratching you'll find something interesting.

In the creative world 'scratching' could involve any of the following:[16]

- A fashion designer visiting vintage stores for inspiration
- A film director flying to an exotic location for new scenes
- A chef digging through piles of international cookbooks for fresh recipes
- A guitarist playing through numerous melodies to find a hook for a song

So if you are short on ideas, expose yourself to new experiences. Don't look for a *big idea* though. Instead, scan widely and freely in order to tease out micro concepts you can build upon.

Being creative isn't as out of reach as artists make it out to be. All you have to do is shuffle, stretch, or scan for new concepts and ideas. Figure 6.1 summarises these principles but if you'd like a more logical approach to the process, check out the exercise at the end of this chapter to learn more.

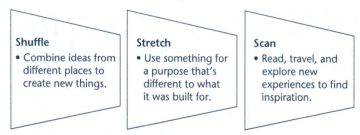

Figure 6.1: The three S's of creativity

A champion for your ideas

Self-belief, passion, endurance, and creativity all contribute to effective entrepreneurship. But there's something missing. Your ideas and efforts will not go far if you can't lead and influence people to support your efforts. For this reason, leadership will be the subject of the next chapter.

Chapter summary

- Creativity is the process of coming up with new, useful ideas.
- It's a vital skill in entrepreneurship because it can help you come up with new business ideas as well as novel solutions to business problems.
- To nurture creativity it's important to be genuinely passionate about what you are doing. It also helps if you don't judge your ideas too early.
- Creative people know that sometimes you just have to create lots of ideas if you want to come up with something incredible. So keep on creating!
- Creative people are also deeply knowledgeable about their work, but they don't allow past experiences to limit what's possible.
- If you want to be more creative, start by mixing unrelated concepts, stretching the applications of things you already know, or exploring new ideas and experiences for inspiration.

📖 Reflection

There are no rules to the creative process. However, if you need some guidance the following steps, first identified by the English psychologist Graham Wallas, can help.[17] Also note that the stages listed below in Figure 6.2 may have to loop over if the ideas you generate aren't worth pursuing.[18]

Exercise: Using the process below, try to come up with a new way of doing something you're interested in. It could be a new laundry service, a t-shirt business, or a way of doing something ordinary more creatively.

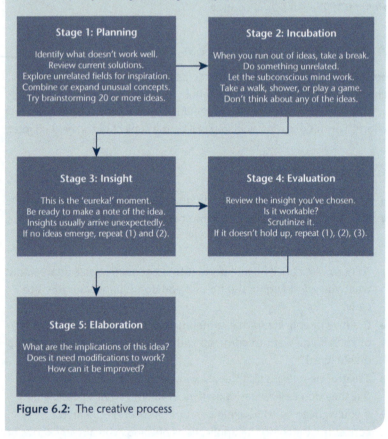

Stage 1: Planning

Identify what doesn't work well.
Review current solutions.
Explore unrelated fields for inspiration.
Combine or expand unusual concepts.
Try brainstorming 20 or more ideas.

Stage 2: Incubation

When you run out of ideas, take a break.
Do something unrelated.
Let the subconscious mind work.
Take a walk, shower, or play a game.
Don't think about any of the ideas.

Stage 3: Insight

This is the 'eureka!' moment.
Be ready to make a note of the idea.
Insights usually arrive unexpectedly.
If no ideas emerge, repeat (1) and (2).

Stage 4: Evaluation

Review the insight you've chosen.
Is it workable?
Scrutinize it.
If it doesn't hold up, repeat (1), (2), (3).

Stage 5: Elaboration

What are the implications of this idea?
Does it need modifications to work?
How can it be improved?

Figure 6.2: The creative process

Useful resources

- Video: *Where Good Ideas Come from* (2010) by Steven Johnson
  https://youtu.be/NugRZGDbPFU

  Why is it worth watching?
  This is a short video that walks you through the evolution of innovative ideas and some of the factors that contribute to creativity.

- Book: *The Creative Habit: Learn It and Use It for Life* (2007) by Twyla Tharp

  Why is it worth reading?
  Written by an award-winning dancer and choreographer, this title shares insights from a wide range of creative domains (film, music, literature, business) and offers plenty of exercises to help boost your creativity.

Leadership

What you will gain from this chapter:

1. Learn about the variety of leadership styles.
2. Understand what leadership is.
3. Appreciate why leadership matters in entrepreneurship.
4. Learn about the qualities of a good leader.

Quiet leadership

What comes to mind when you hear the word 'leadership'? If you've ever been to an assessment day for a graduate job or watched an episode of *The Apprentice*, your view of leadership might be that it's about someone taking charge. A charming but authoritative person usually comes to mind. However, this view of leadership fails to account for the true diversity of leaders. Sometimes leadership isn't so loud. Sometimes it's rather discreet.

Susan Wojcicki (pronounced Whoa-jit-ski) is one example. She's currently a mother of five and was the first woman to have a baby at the company she works for. Her colleagues praise her for being great at recruiting and motivating strong leaders. She also has a way with inspiring confidence in those who work for her. One of the reasons for this is that she credits her team for good work and has no need to massage her ego.

Susan works for two incredibly smart entrepreneurs. But when they go off on a tangent during company meetings she's quick to refocus and challenge them on key priorities. Maybe they listen because many years ago she was once their landlord, charging a little over £1,000 a month for the co-founders to use her garage. The more likely reason, however, is that the company the entrepreneurs started in her house, *Google,* makes most of its money from ideas she developed.[1]

Susan isn't your typical leader. Few people know of her, yet she's the person who spearheaded the development of *Google's* advertising platform, *Adsense*. Susan also led efforts at *Google* to offer better maternity benefits for its female staff.

If you met Susan, you might be surprised at how nice she is. She humorously refers to herself as the 'mom of *Google*'. Today Susan is the CEO of *YouTube* but she remains one of the most understated leaders in the technology business.[2]

Leadership, as exemplified by Susan, doesn't always make the front pages. Sometimes it operates in the background without much attention. But what does it mean to be a leader? Why do entrepreneurs benefit from leadership? And how can you become a better leader? In this chapter we will answer these questions and look at some of the ways you can establish a foundation for effective leadership in business.

 Food for Thought

Can you think of five people who you believe are good leaders? It could be someone famous or it could be someone in your social circle. Make a list, scan through it, and ask yourself, 'what three qualities do these people have that make them good leaders?' Keep these qualities in mind and see if any of them pop up in the rest of the chapter.

Chapter 7

What is leadership?

At its core, leadership is about change. It's a process that energises a group of people to aspire towards an ideal. Charismatic leaders like Barack Obama may get centre stage, but unassuming personalities like the German chancellor Angela Merkel are just as effective.

A leader sets the tone and direction of a venture. They have an idea of what the destination looks like and they guide others towards it. A leader doesn't always resort to coercive means either, in order to influence others. Instead, he or she inspires people through a dream for something better. Leadership doesn't have to be defined by rank, though many think it is. For example, junior staff with expert knowledge can lead senior staff in areas that require specialist knowledge.

Though leadership is complex and dynamic, we know that it always involves a common goal and a group of people determined to reach it. We can therefore define leadership as a process where an individual influences a group to work towards a certain goal.[3]

Leadership in entrepreneurship

If you have an idea for a business, the need for leadership is automatically bestowed upon you. Sure, you can give the idea to someone else and let him or her deal with it. However, if you wish to execute the idea the way you envisioned it, you will naturally have to lead the way. This means that it's important to develop sound leadership abilities if you want to start a new venture.

> **Key term – Leadership:**
> A process where an individual influences a group to work towards a certain goal.

Leadership in entrepreneurship is especially vital in the early stages of a business. It can help you clarify goals and, perhaps just as important, it can inspire others to tag along for the ride. And remember, starting a venture on your own is very difficult so if you can inspire others to help out you'll be at an advantage.[4]

Without solid leadership you risk veering from one direction to the next without really getting anywhere. If you've ever had a boss who couldn't make their mind up about something, you'll know how demotivating such indecisiveness can be.

Poor leadership ultimately leads nowhere. And for a new business it's important that you organise your efforts effectively if you wish to be successful. Leadership can help you achieve this goal. So what can you do to be a better leader? The next section will answer this question.

The three qualities of good leaders

Though great leadership varies in style (for example, some leaders are introverts while others are extroverts), there are three themes that always emerge: vision, values, and virtuosity. These components are evident in all the great leaders that we know.

Take, for example, Martin Luther King. He had an inspiring vision (social justice for all, regardless of race); a bedrock of values (courage, selflessness, non-violence); and virtuosity (he was a talented public speaker). In contrast, a leader without values risks being incongruent: if they change what they stand for all the time, they relinquish their ability to maintain followership. Likewise, a leader without a vision for a better future rarely inspires anyone to join the journey. And finally, a leader who lacks virtuosity (high proficiency at a number of skills that include decisiveness, focus, and knowledge) will find it difficult to garner credibility and respect from his or her followers. Let's now look at each of these components in more detail.

Vision

The Roman philosopher Seneca once remarked that if you don't know where you are sailing, no wind is favourable. This couldn't be any truer in leadership and entrepreneurship. The people you bring to your business will want to have an idea of where you're going. This is why good leaders are often defined by their vision for a better future. One example is the young Nobel Prize winner Malala Yousafzai. Her vision is that every child should have the right to an education. Other examples include Xavier Helgesen and Erica Mackey, two business school graduates whose venture, *Off Grid Electric*, is working to offer renewable and affordable electricity to one million homes in Tanzania

Chapter 7

by 2017.[5] Such visions are compelling and exemplify how great leadership starts with an ideal image of the future.[6]

But what if your dreams aren't so grand? They don't have to be. As long as you have a vision for something inspiring, your efforts can be directed to a clear purpose and this will contribute to the performance of your business.[7]

☑ Tip: What makes a compelling vision

A good place to start in terms of vision is to think about some of the problems you would like to solve, or perhaps some of the ways in which you would like to make the world a better place. But whatever the vision, make sure that it has the following characteristics:

- Brevity – Is it short enough to put into a few sentences?
- Clarity – Is it easy to understand and explain?
- Inspiration – Does it motivate you and your team?

Here are some examples of company visions you might be familiar with:

John Lewis Partnership: *Happiness of all our employees through worthwhile employment in a successful business.*

Google: *To organise the world's information and make it accessible and useful for all.*

L'Oréal: *To offer beauty for all.*

Values

How do you currently make decisions? Are there some things you would never do and others that you are open to? Where does the buck stop? Hopefully you have some values that guide your day-to-day living. As it is, these values may be loose and implicit (e.g. 'I recycle as much as I can') or they may be strict and explicit (e.g. 'I am vegan'). Whatever the values, as long as you have some, life becomes a bit more consistent and easier to navigate.

Effective leadership, too, requires a core set of values – principles or ideals that you stand for. After all, we only follow someone if they stand for something that resonates with us. Equally, we only buy from businesses whose values are in harmony with our own, or at the very least, don't conflict with what we stand for. Here are some examples from the *BBC* website:[9]

- 'Trust is the foundation of the *BBC*: we are independent, impartial, and honest.'
- 'Audiences are at the heart of everything we do.'
- 'We respect each other and celebrate our diversity so that everyone can give their best.'
- 'We are one *BBC*: great things happen when we work together.'

Though it may not be evident at the outset of a new venture, effective business owners are often clear about the values they stand for. So you have to reflect on the ideas you value and consider whether they can be imbued in your business as well. But a word of caution: what matters isn't whether you stick to the values 100 percent of the time. What matters is that you make your best efforts to adhere to them.

Virtuosity

Effective leadership also stems from having great skill in a number of areas. This enables a leader to not only direct efforts in a new venture, but to also add value in a meaningful way. In addition, the more developed these competences are the more legitimacy and respect you'll earn from a team.[9]

What are the skills and competencies that you need? It depends on the individual and the business. Generally you need to be proficient at something that is valuable to your venture. Ben Cohen and Jerry Greenfield, for example, completed an ice cream-making course before creating *Ben & Jerry's*. The course was a 'distance learning' programme and cost the equivalent of just £10.[10] On the other hand, Steve Jobs didn't know how to build a computer but he had a knack for business and teamed up with the legendary engineer Steve Wozniak to build the first *Apple* machine.

Apart from the necessary knowledge that's specific to your venture (i.e. 'domain expertise'), there are a number of other general skills that effective leaders need to be good at. These include being decisive, having the ability to focus on what matters, being a good communicator, and being good with people. An illustrative summary of this skillset is provided in Table 7.1.

Table 7.1: General skills of an effective leader

Decision making
- Do you make decisions promptly or do you procrastinate by trying to find all the facts?
- Do you consider more than one view?
- Do you seek feedback after you've made a decision?

Focus
- Have you identified your priorities and are you working on them?
- Are you focusing on what you can control rather than what you can't?
- Are you measuring progress?

Communication
- Can you communicate objectives clearly?
- Are you good at public speaking?
- Do you communicate frequently enough?

People
- Can you motivate people?
- Do you understand your own strengths and weaknesses?
- Can you spot talents (and shortcomings) in other people?

All the skills in Table 7.1 contribute to virtuosity in leadership – the mastery of skills that will help you realise your vision. If you are weak in any of these areas, be sure to take steps to develop them.

In conclusion, effective leadership is driven by a compelling vision, consistent values, and skills that are relevant to a venture. If you cultivate these themes in your entrepreneurial journey, you will become a better leader and entrepreneur.

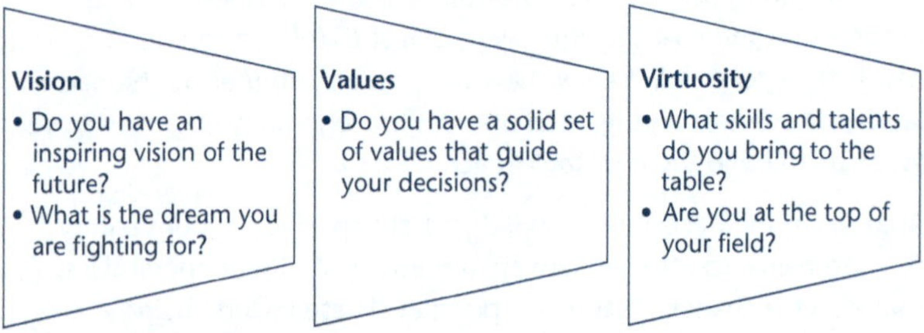

Vision
- Do you have an inspiring vision of the future?
- What is the dream you are fighting for?

Values
- Do you have a solid set of values that guide your decisions?

Virtuosity
- What skills and talents do you bring to the table?
- Are you at the top of your field?

Figure 7.1: Themes of effective leadership

⌘ Entrepreneur's Insight
Elizabeth Galbut, founding partner of SoGal Ventures

Elizabeth is a high-achieving graduate who went on to co-found the first female-led millennial investment firm in the USA. She makes an important point about leadership:

> So my words of advice are that first of all, not everyone has to be a captain of a ship. So know yourself personally. Are you a better captain or are you a better second mate? And being a great second mate is very honourable and very wonderful as well. So not everyone has to be the CEO. You can also be a co-founder.

Chapter summary

- Leadership is the ability to influence a group to work together for a common goal.
- Good leadership matters in entrepreneurship because it helps clarify objectives and focuses efforts when creating a new venture.
- To be an effective leader you must have vision, values, and virtuosity.
- Vision is an ideal image of the future. This is what will inspire the team.
- Values guide your work and enable your efforts to be more congruent.
- Virtuosity makes you a more effective entrepreneur. It also helps you build credibility and legitimacy. This involves good industry knowledge, sound decision-making, clear communication, focus, and excellent people skills.

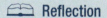 **Reflection**

Think back to a time when you demonstrated leadership qualities. Maybe you were a captain for a sports team, a committee member of a society at university, or a seasoned blogger on a niche topic. How well do you think you demonstrated the following?

- Vision
  - What were your goals?
  - Were your aims clearly defined or vague?

- Values
  - What did you stand for?
  - Did you communicate your values to your team?

- Virtuosity
  - What skills were pivotal to your success?
  - Did you become proficient at a skill that was valuable to the team?

In light of the above and before starting a business, try to consider the following: What vision do you have for your venture? What values will it abide by? What skills will you have to develop to be an effective entrepreneur and leader? You can answer these questions after reading the rest of the book or make a note of some early ideas now.

Useful resources

- Book: *Leadership: Plain and Simple* (2012) by Steve Radcliffe

  Why is it worth reading?
  This is a no-nonsense guide to leadership that is free from business jargon and clichés. The book is simple but not dumbed down and will advance your leadership development further.

Skill set

In Part 1 of the book we came to appreciate the makings of an entrepreneurial mindset. Effective entrepreneurs believe in themselves; they have a passion for what they do; they endure in the face of obstacles; they are creative; and most of all they are leaders.

In Part 2 we will turn to the fundamental skills of an entrepreneur. We will look at strategy, marketing, sales, branding, and finance. This list is not exhaustive and does not cover all the topics required to start a business. However, it gives you a fantastic place to start as you embark on the journey to create your own business.

Strategy

What you will gain from this chapter:

1. Learn about the origins of strategy.
2. Know what strategy means and why it's valuable.
3. Be able to use strategy in your ventures.

The face that launched a thousand ships

Strategy has its roots in ancient warfare. The battlefield is replete with examples of the craft but perhaps none are more telling than the legend of Helen of Troy.

In the myth, the world's most handsome man, Paris of Troy, ran off with the world's most beautiful woman, Helen of Sparta. However, the affair turned out to be fatal since Helen was already married to the king of Sparta, Menelaus. Angered by the event, Menelaus formed an alliance with other Greek kingdoms and set out to punish the Trojans. The furious king launched a thousand ships and set out on a war that would last for a decade.

Why is this story so interesting with regards to strategy? What's fascinating is that the combined Greek forces had a larger army, but for nearly ten years the city of Troy could not be defeated. Legend has it that it was the walls – built by the gods Apollo and Poseidon – that gave the Trojans their edge. And no matter how much force the Greeks used, they couldn't barge into the city.

It wasn't until the tenth year that the Greeks decided to employ a different strategy. Instead of using brute force to gain access to the city they would attempt to open the gates from the inside. To do so, the Greeks built the famous Trojan horse – a gigantic wooden figure that was devised to take advantage of the Trojans' curiosity.

The strategy paid off. When the Trojans discovered the horse they captured it and brought it back to their city. They thought that the horse would bring them luck but unbeknown to them it concealed a small group of Greek soldiers. While the Trojans were sleeping, the hidden Greek warriors crept out of the horse, opened the gates of Troy, and a fleet of Greek soldiers who were waiting outside overwhelmed the city.

This story highlights the power of being artful in finding hidden advantages. This is what strategy is about. And even though it originates from conflict,[1] strategic thinking is now employed in a wide range of peaceful domains, including entrepreneurship.

Being strategic gives us a chance where we might not otherwise have one. It enables us to be more tactful in how we go about things and can tip the odds in our favour when we don't have enough resources. But what exactly is strategy? What strategic principles should you keep in mind when starting or running a business? We will turn to these questions next.

 Food for Thought

Can you see how strategy links with creativity? Sometimes the most obvious path is the least effective and we have to think divergently if we want to be successful. If you have a business idea in mind, can you think of ways you can execute it in a strategically advantageous manner? Don't worry if nothing comes to mind. The following sections will help you get your strategic hat on.

What is strategy?

In ancient Athens, army generals used to have the title 'strategos', which is a compound of two words: 'stratos' (army) and 'agein' (to lead). To be an effective strategos one had to be crafty, straightforward, loving, tough, and full of energy. You were also required to have good leadership skills, political acumen, and practical intelligence.[2] Such is the history from which the word *strategy* is derived. But what does strategy mean in the 21st century?

If you google the word 'strategy' it's easy to get lost. More than 90 formal definitions have been published in the last 40 years alone and, despite being a hot topic, strategy is one of the least understood concepts in business.[3] However, this does not mean that the concept can't be grasped. We can define strategy quite simply as follows: strategy is the art of creating an advantage.

In business, strategy is a combination of commitments, decisions, and actions that will give you an edge.[4] Strategy guides your choices in all of the following matters:

- Products or services you want to make
- Customers you would like to target
- The means or tactics you use to attract customers (but note: tactics are the small actions you make on a daily basis; strategy is what they amount to)

> **Key term – Strategy:**
> The art of creating an advantage.

Strategy is what you choose to *do,* as much as what you choose *not* to do. In some ways strategy can also be defined as the art of creating power.[5] But in more general terms, strategy is figuring out what you want to achieve and how you can increase your odds of success.

Strategy in entrepreneurship

When thinking about your business idea and what to do after university, a strategic mindset will help you clarify thoughts, plans, and actions. On average, good strategies contribute to better business performance.[6] Let's look at some of the reasons why this is.

Chapter 8

Resourcefulness

When you start a business, you probably won't have all the resources that you need. But as the poet Homer would say, a determined strategist knows how to win with lesser horses. Thinking strategically helps you work more economically and also inspires you to seek advantages you may otherwise overlook.

In practice, a poor strategist tries to do everything on his or her own. A good strategist, on the other hand, knows that you are better off leveraging the skills or resources of others if you are weak or unresourceful in other areas.

Impact

As well as being resourceful, strategic thinking can help you increase the impact of your efforts. This is because good strategists are able to identify the most critical parts of a challenge. They apply efforts where results are likely to be most fruitful.

In practice, a poor strategist spends months crafting the world's greatest marketing scheme while doing little to develop a good product. In contrast, a good strategist will first try to understand if anyone needs his or her product before spending lots of time on marketing.

Consistency

A clear strategy drives the choices you make in a business. It provides consistency and helps you solidify your reputation, brand image, and credibility in the marketplace.[7]

In practice, a poor strategist may start a business that specifically targets wealthy customers, yet he or she may use very cheap materials to save costs and make more profits. However, a good strategist knows that first impressions count and in catering to wealthy people, quality should be a priority.

Avoiding zero-sum contests

Strategy was born out of warfare but even then the aim was to find ways of winning with less bloodshed, not more. It's no different in business except that bloodshed comes in the form of business losses. Business strategy therefore involves thinking of ways you can compete effectively without amassing significant losses.

In practice, a poor strategist will take on the competition head-to-head. They will compete on just prices until there's hardly any profit left in the marketplace. A great strategist knows better. Instead of offering a product or service in exactly the same way as a competitor does, they will position themselves differently and offer the customer something unique.

⌘ **Entrepreneur's Insight**
Anna Pinder, co-founder of Lunch Bxd

Anna is the co-founder of the food start-up *Lunch Bxd*. They specialise in delivering fresh salad boxes in central London. Here's what she had to say when asked about the competition:

> There are some businesses doing similar [things] but not exactly the same. Since we started last year we've seen a lot more spring up. Obviously you've got the big companies like Pret and M&S who do deliveries to the offices. And then there's the companies that do hot food deliveries. But a lot of them are focused more on dinner and delivering to people's homes rather than delivering to offices. And ours are salads, so it's obviously a cold meal. So there's no actual direct competition as such. Which is good and slightly different.

Preparedness

Finally, strategy encourages big-picture thinking. This prevents you from getting lost in the detail and going off-course if certain actions aren't getting you closer to big-picture objectives. Strategy also involves the anticipation of several scenarios, so you are better prepared for opportunities or threats that may emerge later on (the pre-mortem concept we encountered in Chapter 5 is a great example of this).

In practice, a poor strategist may open a business and not anticipate how they will deal with the competition. When a rival enters the market the poor strategist panics and tries to compete on price. On the other hand, a good strategist anticipates competition. When a rival emerges, a good strategist is prepared and knows how to deal with the opposition.

 Food for Thought

Think back to when you applied to university or when you applied for graduate jobs. Did you employ strategic thinking or did you take a more haphazard approach? If you took the second option, in what ways could you have done things better? If the answers are unclear, don't worry. In the next section we will review principles of strategy you can use in business and life.

Principles of strategy

In entrepreneurship you always have to think strategically. If you run out of cash you will need to think of ways you can do more with less. If people aren't responding well to your product or service you will need to dig deep to uncover the real issues at play. And when someone else copies your idea you will have to be prepared to respond effectively and decisively. All these actions require good strategic thinking and in order to do that you need:

- Insight (as opposed to blind meandering)
- Mētis or ingenuity (as opposed to assuming conventions)
- Focus (as opposed to trying to do lots of different things)
- Versatility (as opposed to being rigid)

Let's look at each of these principles in a bit more detail.

Insight

Strategic thinking begins with insight – a deep understanding of issues relevant to your situation. For instance, as an entrepreneur you will need to consider both internal and external issues.

Internal issues relate to your own strengths and weaknesses and it's important to be self-aware in this regard. This is because there are times when a weakness could be used as a strength, and vice-versa.

For example, when the rental car company *Avis* wanted to increase its market share in the 1960s it decided to use its weakness (a lower market share) against the market leader, *Hertz*. *Avis* achieved this by running advertising campaigns with the following copy:

> 66 When you're only No. 2, you try harder. 99

The campaign was a huge success. *Avis* grew its market share as customers started to appreciate that because the company was not in first place, it would not rest on its laurels. Thanks to the campaign *Avis* eventually turned a loss-making business into a profit-making enterprise.[8] But several years later *Hertz* fought back:

> 66 For years, Avis has been telling you Hertz is No. 1.
> Now we're going to tell you why. 99

This example demonstrates how an acute awareness of your strengths and weaknesses can be advantageous. With such knowledge you can craft more consistent and intelligent strategies, just as *Avis* and *Hertz* did in the example above.

You can also glean insights from external issues. Here's one example. There's a saying: a rising tide lifts all boats. This is especially relevant for entrepreneurs analysing the external world because if you can spot a 'rising tide' – trends and changes in the economy, society, or technology – you can build a business that will take advantage of them. However, you will also have to keep watch for emerging threats that could negatively affect your venture.

 Food for Thought

Did you know that in a recession people spend more on feel-good products and services? Beauty items, personal care products, as well as comfort eating, all take off.[9] Can you think of another 'rising tide' that could benefit or impact a business? Here are some more examples:

- Health-conscious society – there's a growing demand for healthy food options in the restaurant sector.

- Smart phones – a lot of Internet browsing happens on mobile devices so customers expect mobile-friendly websites.
- Privacy – people want to be confident that businesses won't misuse customer email addresses and other digital data.

Mētis

Strategy was created because ingenuity could achieve what brute force could not. The Greeks had a term for such cleverness: *mētis*. It is a timeless principle of strategy that is worth employing in entrepreneurship.

Mētis is all about being resourceful under pressure. It's a practical sort of intelligence that seeks out advantages in hidden places.[10] When the Greeks changed their strategy to opening the gates of Troy from the inside, they were using mētis. When a young entrepreneur invents a cure for hiccups by using a lollipop that over-stimulates the very nerves that cause the ailment,[11] she's using mētis.

A good strategy – whether it's marketing, product, or finance related – often looks beyond the obvious. In some ways it may even be oblique. That is to say, whatever your objective is, a good strategy sometimes takes the path less travelled.

Focus

Another element of strategy that's especially crucial is focus. Broad goals, vague objectives, and conflicting ideas about what you are trying to achieve in your business are a recipe for disaster. On the other hand, if you focus your efforts in a co-ordinated and targeted capacity you increase the effectiveness of your actions.[12]

Take advertising for example. When starting a new business you may be tempted to market your business to as many people as you can. However, if you follow this path you will also waste efforts on people who don't need your product or service. As we will learn in Chapter 9, a more strategic approach would be to focus on a smaller group of people who have a deep need or appreciation for your business. So whatever your goals or objectives are, it helps to keep them tight and focused.

☑ **Tip: Creating a competitive business strategy**

Strategic thinking can be applied in marketing, finance, sales, and a range of other business areas. But in the early stages it's also useful to have an overall generic strategy[13] for your venture. The ideas in Table 8.1 are a good starting point.

Table 8.1: Generic competitive strategies

Cost Leadership	Differentiation	Focus
• **Strategy:** Offer the best prices to customers. • **How:** By negotiating better prices with suppliers or investing in equipment that can achieve cost savings. • **Comment:** Difficult to achieve in a small business unless you can buy in bulk or invest in special equipment that produces a product cheaply.	• **Strategy:** Offer a unique product, service, or experience. • **How:** Can be achieved through superior customer service or a unique product or experience. • **Comment:** Easier for new businesses since it doesn't require big upfront costs. You just have to be creative.	• **Strategy:** Focus on a specific type of customer or a particular subset of products. • **How:** By focusing on a group of people within a certain demographic, or a niche product (for example, golf balls). • **Comment:** Helps you specialise and through this you become better differentiated and may also achieve better prices.

When thinking about your business, try to focus on just one of these strategies. This is because if you keep switching between approaches you will confuse customers, waste resources, and perform worse than businesses that have clarity about their aims.

Versatility

What separates strategy from mere planning is that it adapts to new circumstances. A business plan may help you articulate what you hope to achieve but if it's lacking in strategic guidance it won't be of much use when new opportunities or threats emerge. Admiral Lord Nelson, the iconic 18th century British naval commander, knew this all too well. In a battle against the French, instead of using flag signals to direct his fleet, Nelson ignored convention and instead offered his crew one strategic principle:

> 66 Whatever you do, get alongside an enemy ship. 99

This command meant that even in the dark, when flag signals were useless, Nelson's crew knew exactly what to do: get close to an enemy ship and engage it one-on-one! Meanwhile the crew were free to choose whatever tactic would achieve this aim.[14]

☑ Tip: Signs of a poor strategy

- Lacks knowledge and insight.
- Assumes conventional means are the best way forward.
- Tries to achieve lots of things without any particular priorities.
- Fails to adapt to new opportunities or threats.

As an entrepreneur, you will also need flexible principles to guide your venture. For example, if one of your business goals is to help people improve their health and you wish to achieve this through a range of healthy snacks, try to also be open to other opportunities. You may learn, for instance, that people are more interested in your recipes and lifestyle advice. If this avenue appears promising you can pivot from a food business into a lifestyle health business. This is what versatility is about. It involves keeping an eye on the prize but being open to the different roads that can get you to your destination.

Chapter summary

- Strategy is the art of creating an advantage. It's about how you can increase your chances of success in an unpredictable world.
- In business, strategy is a combination of objectives, choices, and actions that give you an edge.
- Strategy matters in business because it helps you become more resourceful, impactful, and consistent in your efforts.
- No matter what your strategy is, it should be based on insight, mētis (ingenuity), focus, and versatility.
- Before you start your venture, it helps if you can identify an overall business strategy. This will either be based on cost leadership, differentiation, or focus.

Useful resources

- Movie: *Moneyball* (2011) starring Brad Pitt and Jonah Hill

  Why is it worth watching?
  How do you create a winning baseball team with a tight budget? Watch this movie to see how an underdog with a great strategy can defeat titans.

- Video: *What is Strategy?* (2015) by BYU Marriott School of Management
  https://youtu.be/TD7WSLeQtVw

  Why is it worth watching?
  This video reinforces the basics of business strategy. It also provides guidance on how to formulate a good strategy and shares a practical example.

- Book: *Playing to Win: How Strategy Really Works* (2013) by A. G. Lafley and Roger L. Martin

  Why is it worth reading?
  This is a more detailed look at strategy from two seasoned businessmen (including the ex-CEO of *Proctor and Gamble*). It is more applicable to larger businesses but if you are ambitious and wish to learn more, this is a good place to start.

Marketing

What you will gain from this chapter:

1. Understand why marketing matters.
2. Be able to define marketing.
3. Have knowledge about the basic principles of marketing.

The world's first road trip

You may not know who Bertha Ringer is but in 1888 she pulled off one of the world's first marketing stunts for a car business. How did this come to be? It all started in 1869 when a 20-year-old Bertha fell in love with an introverted engineer. And, though he was a clever man, he was hopeless at business. He lacked self-belief and would often doubt himself. Bertha thought differently. She believed in the engineer so much that when his workshop almost went bust she did not hesitate to invest her dowry and inheritance in order to save the business. Who was the lucky chap? It was none other than Carl Benz, founder of *Mercedes-Benz* and the man Bertha would eventually marry.[1]

In 1886 Carl had invented the world's first automobile. But despite years of effort and a compelling product, only a few people were interested. The general public did not believe the invention was reliable and many went as far as to think that a car was the work of the devil.[2] Kaiser Wilhelm II, the last German emperor, protested:

> ❝I believe in the horse. The automobile is nothing more than a passing phenomenon… As long as I have warm horses, I will never sit in these stinking carts.[3]❞

It's not hard to imagine that Carl Benz was demoralised by such a reception. But while his vision for the future was crushed by such disinterest, his wife did not lose faith. She still believed that human travel could be transformed with Carl's invention. She just needed to articulate the future of travel in a new way.

Undeterred by what the public thought of her husband's work, Bertha devised a brilliant marketing stunt that would not only encourage her husband but also prove to the world how capable the automobile was. And so, on an early summer's day in 1888 Bertha snuck out of the house with her two sons and left a note for Carl. The message she left was a white lie. She wrote that she was taking the children to see their grandmother some 56 miles away. However, she didn't mention that they were going to use the Benz Motor Car, a vehicle that was still in need of development.

The car had no fuel tank other than a 4.5-litre supply in the engine components. It had just two forward gears, no clutch or modern footbrake, and could only achieve a top speed of 10 mph. Roads as we know them today were also non-existent. But despite these challenges Bertha believed that the journey was possible. So she set out on what would become the world's first long-distance trip in a car.[4]

The journey turned out to be a success. News of the woman who travelled more than 100 miles with two children in the Motor Car soon spread across Germany and sceptics of the invention turned into advocates. Bertha's journey generated lots of publicity and her stunt paved the way for *Mercedes-Benz* to become the largest car company in the world by the end of the 19th century.[5]

Without Bertha's marketing ploy, mass adoption of cars would have been slower. Indeed, if no one is captivated by a message or story about a product or service, it can be difficult to get customers. Therefore, marketing is a crucial step in starting and running a business and in this chapter, we will look at how you can use the skill to your advantage. But first we need to define marketing and then consider what effective marketing requires.

What is marketing?

Marketing is a wide-ranging discipline. There are thousands of books on the topic and several definitions of the term. For instance, one textbook defines marketing as follows:

> ❝ The process by which companies create value for customers and build strong customer relationships in order to capture value from customers in return.[6] ❞

In this book we will stick to a definition that is a bit more concrete. In light of this, marketing can be defined as the process of identifying, attracting, and retaining customers. Each of these steps has its own branch of knowledge that goes beyond the scope of this book. However, we will briefly touch on each, with special emphasis on how to attract customers.

Effective marketing

Marketing is effective when you identify, attract, and retain customers profitably. This boils down to the following:

1. Identify customers you would like to sell to. (The more specific the better. More on this later.)
2. Develop something those customers find valuable. (If there's no real value, customers who initially buy from you won't come back.)
3. Communicate your value using the most potent means possible. (If your message has no impact, no one will buy from you. Remember the Bertha Benz story!)

These three steps simplify marketing but the list is sufficient to get you acquainted with the topic as you start a new venture. Furthermore, it's worth noting the following general pattern: you can have an amazing product but if you can't communicate its worth, your marketing effectiveness falls to zero. On the other hand, a compelling message with a dud of a product also drives marketing effectiveness down to zero. Therefore, the right balance lies in having a valuable product and a compelling message. This is what marketing effectiveness is all about.

But what about the specifics, you may ask. The next section will share actionable marketing advice you can use when you start your business.

> ## ⌘ Entrepreneur's Insight
> ## Naomi Twigden, co-founder of Lunch Bxd
>
> How do you market a brand-new salad box delivery business? Naomi from *Lunch Bxd* shares her early experience below:
>
> > *At the beginning we did a few days of flyering. Just me and Anna [the co-founder] and we got a friend to design something for us and we just went and handed out flyers outside. Actually I think we stood outside Pret! So we did that for two days at the beginning and that's how we got our first few customers, which is quite cool. And then people saw our lunch boxes in the offices, so we got more customers through that. [The boxes] look different because it's in a brown box. It's not in a brown bag, so it looks different from what you normally see. We then made a website right from the start and sent out newsletters and built up people on that, offering discounts, and sending through menus. We've also always done a lot of social media and send samples out to magazines and food blogs.*

Principles of marketing

Marketing comes first

Marketing should not start after your business has launched. It's a process that should unfold the moment you decide to explore a business opportunity. Once you know what problem you are solving (we discuss this in Chapter 13), and who for, you should then design your product or service in a way that will attract and retain customers.

As a rule of thumb, avoid creating a product first and then thinking about marketing ideas at later stages. Instead, introduce marketing concepts into your offering at the earliest development stage. This way, your product will do more than satisfy your customers. It will also market itself from the get-go.

> **Key term – Marketing:**
> The process of identifying, attracting, and retaining customers.

Start with a niche market

Marketing involves being selective about your market. A market is just a group of potential customers who all have a common set of needs or wants.[7] What kind of market should you pick? It will depend on what your business has to offer. But if you are just starting out, it's good practice to choose a small, passionate minority over a large, neutral majority. This is important for the following reasons.

First, if you try to please everyone you end up delighting no one. This is because in order to please the majority, you have to tone down what would excite a niche group just to avoid putting off a dispassionate majority. In other words, you have to make your business average if you want to cater to the masses. But who talks about an average business? Nobody. And to make matters worse, working to the concept of average is sometimes nonsensical. For example, there are almost two and a half people per household in the UK[8] but you will never find a house with half a human being. So in marketing you are better off starting with a small but precise group of people who you know will be delighted to consume your product or service. These are the people who will generate word-of-mouth recommendations for your business. Not the silent majority.

Second, in the early stages of your business you are likely to be short on resources. However, if you focus on a small segment of customers you can execute your business idea more effectively. For example, a restaurant with 100 items on the menu may have something for everyone but it will cost more to set up. Not only that but such a restaurant won't be able to attract vegan customers if a specialist vegan restaurant opens next door. Which brings us to the final reason why you should start with a niche market.

Consider this example. If you were looking for new running shoes, what brand would you go for? Speak to anyone who's passionate about running and you'll likely hear about *ASICS*. The company has been around longer than *Nike* and has been making running shoes since the 1950s. It's a leader in running shoes and having a specialist focus helps them stand out. A relevant analogy here is that *ASICS* is like a big fish in a small pond rather than a small fish in a big pond. Moreover, the benefit of starting with a niche market is that you get to be a big fish sooner. You will also find it easier to maintain your position as a leader when your pond gets bigger.[9]

⌘ **Entrepreneur's Insight**
Dr Sam Decombel, CSO and co-founder
of FitnessGenes

FitnessGenes offers nutrition and fitness advice based on your genetic profile. Where did they start? Co-founder and Chief Scientific Officer Dr Sam Decombel sheds light on her venture's genesis below:

> *We started off very much with the body-building niche, which was right for us. Small businesses need to be really targeted given the limited resources that you have in advertising. So that suited us perfectly and it allowed us to build a very significant customer base and very loyal customer base in that market... Now, there's a much wider application for this technology for personalised training and diet plans which is in this area [of] the problem that we have in Western society with obesity and ill health, particularly into old age... So we've gone from building what was essentially a product aimed at body builders, to looking at a much more wider-reaching technology that could hopefully impact some fairly significant issues that we as a population in the West are facing over the next 20 to 50 years.*

☑ **Tip: Focus on passionate groups**

Marketing for a new business should focus on a small group of people who really care about a particular product or service. You can identify these people by the following characteristics:[10]

● Their friends look to them for advice.

> ☑ **Tip: (Continued)**
>
> - They like trying new things.
> - They want to be the first to have or use something new.
> - They don't like the status quo.
> - They are more forgiving of early faults since they are happy to be the first to use or consume something new.
>
> This is the minority you should market to in the early stages of your business. They're the ones who can kick-start a trend. If you can't do well with these customers you probably won't do well with the mass market.

Build a remarkable business

Shreddies Coco Caramel, Froot Loops Bloopers, Special K Chocolate and Strawberry, Cheerios Honey Nut Medley Crunch. These are just some of the 120 types of cereals that *Cereal Killer Café*, the UK's first cereal restaurant, have on offer. Founded by two hipster-bearded twins, the café and its founders don't need to do much to stand out. They're remarkable.

Marie Kondo is in the business of decluttering. Her consulting business in Tokyo, which she started at the age of 19, helps people transform their rooms for the better. You would think that this was a small lifestyle business. Quite the contrary. She has a three-month waiting list of clients and her book, *The Life-Changing Magic of Tidying Up*, has sold more than two million copies to date. Kondo's method of tidying is extreme: get rid of anything that doesn't spark 'joy'. Is her business ordinary? No. It is remarkable? Yes.

In the world of marketing these examples are often referred to as 'purple cows', a term coined by marketer Seth Godin. He describes the concept as follows: when you drive past a farm full of brown cows you don't take any notice. But if there's a purple cow in the mix you take notice and tell all your friends about it. This is the effect you are looking for when you start a business. You want to make sure that you build something that's worth talking about (see Table 9.1).

Table 9.1: Principles of a remarkable business

Principle	Examples
1. Create Something New – Don't try to beat the competition by offering something marginally better. Instead, create something new.	*Red Bull* was the first energy drinks business and they've continued to dominate the category for decades.
2. Reach for the Edges – Your business should be exceptional at something. That's what gets people talking, outliers. So you can be super-fast, super-cheap, super-sized, or super-small, but never ordinary. Remarkable companies reach for the edges and so should you.[11]	*Zappos.com* reaches for the edges. The business is based on superior customer service. If you are unhappy with a purchase, you have a whole year to return it. The company also goes to the extremes when hiring. To ensure that only the most passionate members of staff are retained, the company offers $2,000 to new hires should they wish to quit. Fewer than 2 percent of recruits take up the offer.
3. Be Focused – People find it easier to remember businesses that stand for a few things rather than everything. If you try to become a jack of all trades no one will remember you. But if your business can own a word or concept in people's minds, your venture will be far more memorable.[12]	What comes to mind when you think of 'ethical cosmetics'? Most people will say *The Body Shop*. (Note: most businesses that create a new category also tend to own the label of that bracket.) How about if you're moving into a new apartment and are looking for 'affordable furniture'? *IKEA* usually tops the list.

Chapter 9

Craft contagious messages

At the heart of marketing is communication. Without it no one will know about you. Moreover, there's so much competing for attention these days that you have to be very crafty with your messages. So just like your business, your communication has to be remarkable. It should be refreshing, exceptional, and targeted to a specific audience. Not only that, it also needs to be a message that can spread. It needs to be contagious.

> ☑ **Tip: Viral marketing checklist**[13]
>
> - Is your message surprising, unusual, or novel?
> - Does it arouse people and drive them to action through awe, excitement, anger, or anxiety?
> - Is the message connected to your business or an idea that you stand for?

Have you seen a *Blendtec* video? If not, you're in the minority. *Blendtec* manufactures blenders and the business rose to prominence thanks to a series of viral videos. In each clip a mad scientist (played by the company's founder Tom Dickson) poses the question: will it blend? He then proceeds to blend anything from an iPad to golf balls. Whatever the item, it's reduced to dust by the end of the video. The clips are extraordinary, entertaining, and worthy of a remark. How contagious are *Blendtec's* videos? They've been viewed more than 100 million times and have boosted sales by 700 percent.[14]

Contagious messages don't require big budgets either. *Blendtec's* original 'Will it Blend?' video cost just $50 to produce. Nonetheless, for your message to spread you have to craft it in a way that will inspire people to share it.

Chapter summary

- Marketing is the process of identifying, attracting, and retaining customers profitably.
- To be effective at marketing you need to be clear about your target customers; you need to have a valuable proposition; and you need to communicate your worth.
- Try not to leave marketing until after you've launched your business. Instead, aim to design a business that's worth talking about.
- Remarkable businesses usually create new things or reach for the edges by excelling at a particular activity. To create a business worth talking about, do either or both of these things.
- When it comes to communicating the value of your business, make sure that your message is contagious and that it is something people will remember.

Useful resources

- Book: *The 22 Immutable Laws of Marketing (1994)* by Al Ries and Jack Trout

  Why is it worth reading?
  The book is more than 20 years old but has stood the test of time. It includes several marketing principles that are still applicable today. The book is a good place to start if you are new to marketing.

- Book: *Growth Hacker Marketing: A Primer on the Future of PR, Marketing and Advertising* (2014) by Ryan Holiday

  Why is it worth reading?
  Despite the techy title, this book is also a fantastic resource for people who are new to marketing. It has the added benefit of offering tactics that are especially relevant to entrepreneurs in a world dominated by technology. As such, this is a must-read for anyone looking to employ the latest thinking in marketing.

Sales

What you will gain from this chapter:

1. Appreciate the value of selling skills in business and in life.
2. Understand selling in the context of entrepreneurship.
3. Learn the pre-requisites to a successful sale.
4. Acquire the key principles of selling.

The sales interview question

In the final scene of the 2013 movie *The Wolf of Wall Street*, Jordan Belfort (played by Leonardo DiCaprio) is introduced at a seminar as the world's greatest sales trainer. No longer one to exude arrogance, Belfort thanks the audience, takes centre stage, and pauses for a moment. For a while his intent is unclear. But just as the audience start to become restless, Belfort casually walks over to a man in the front row and offers him a classic sales litmus test: 'sell me this pen'.

The challenge is legendary in sales circles; some employers use it as a prompt when interviewing candidates for sales jobs. This is because it can demonstrate how good someone is at selling.

Take a moment to think about the challenge. How would you respond? Pick up a pen or any small item nearby and give it a go. Don't worry if it is difficult or awkward. Simply do what comes naturally to you. Try it for one minute then return to the following paragraph.

How did you find the experience? Did you use any of the following (or similar) statements?

- 'You should buy this pen. It's a fantastic pen for business people... you'll like it.'
- 'You can use the pen to write letters, it has lots of ink and lasts for a long time, you will love it.'
- 'I'll sell you this pen at a bargain price. You like pens don't you? Here, try it out. It's the best pen I've ever seen.'

Would you be convinced by any of these statements if you were a customer? Probably not. But that's how most people try to sell and it often gets them nowhere. Fortunately, this chapter will help you do better.

In the following sections we will look at what selling really is, why it matters in entrepreneurship, how to prepare for the process, and the principles you can adopt to improve your sales ability.

What is sales?

What comes to mind when you think of a salesperson? How about the idea of 'selling' in general? Unfortunately, some of us feel uneasy about these concepts. We think back to a few bad experiences we've had with salespeople and squirm at the thought of ever having to *sell* anything.

This view is somewhat justified. We are all familiar with the fast-talking salesperson who will flog you something at a bargain price only for it to break down a few weeks later; the cold callers who try to sell you insurance, utilities, and a variety of other no-win-no-fee products that you aren't interested in; not to mention the hagglers who won't budge on price but will happily 'upsell' you items you don't need. Now also imagine being the salesperson that absolutely *needs* to 'close' a sale because their livelihood depends on it.

All these examples are a caricature of sales. And in each of the above cases, it is a process that has gone wrong. So what is good selling really about?

Defining Sales

Selling is the process of turning prospects into customers. Prospects are people who are likely to find value in what you have to offer. Sometimes prospects know what they want and you don't have to do much 'selling' (e.g. a hungry person walking into a restaurant to buy food). And at other times prospects don't really know what their needs are. In the latter scenario the sales process can be more elaborative and it is the duty of a salesperson to learn more about a prospect and determine whether the product or service being sold can provide value to them.

Selling can also have a broader scope. While 10 percent of the working population are employed in traditional sales jobs,[1] a study by Daniel Pink and the research firm *Qualtrics* found that many of us are more involved in selling than we realise. On average, around 40 percent of our working time is spent persuading, influencing, and convincing other people to give up something in exchange for what we have to offer.[2] Pink refers to this process as 'non-sales selling'. Examples include when we sell ourselves in interviews, on social media, or even to the girl or boy we'd like to date.

In this wider view, selling can be defined as a process of persuading someone to give you his or her resources (e.g. cash or time) in exchange for something you have to offer. Just how important is this process when it comes to starting a business? The rest of this chapter will answer that question and provide guidance on how you can excel at selling.

> ## ⌘ Entrepreneur's Insight
> ## Bob Etherington, founder of Etherington Group
>
> *It doesn't matter what business you have, whether you're a dentist, whether you're a lawyer, whether you're a software designer, if you can't sell, you don't have a business. Because without selling nothing else happens.*

Entrepreneurship and selling

In the previous chapter we learnt that marketing helps generate interest in your business. However, it is *selling* that converts that interest into cash. Out of all the entrepreneurial skills, selling is perhaps the most critical and pervasive. Indeed, a venture can only turn into a business if you can convince prospects to part with their cash in exchange for what you have to offer.

> **Key term – Selling:**
> The process of turning prospects into customers.

When done properly, selling helps others realise the value of your product or service. That value may or may not be relevant to their personal circumstances, but without selling it is impossible to tell.

If we take the broader definition of selling – that is, persuading others to part with their resources in exchange for yours – you will find that as a founder, you have to sell your business idea when recruiting co-founders and teammates, when looking for investment, when dealing with suppliers, partners, and potential distributors. So not only do you have to sell to customers, you also have to sell your ideas to the rest of the world.

Selling is a very broad topic and depending on whom you're selling to – whether it's to Joe and Jenny down the road (business-to-consumer selling), or to a local company (business-to-business selling) – you may have to employ different tactics. Likewise, the way you sell or pitch your idea to investors will be different from how you sell it when looking for a co-founder.

While specific approaches for various sales scenarios are beyond the scope of this book, the next section considers key sales principles you can use to become a better salesperson. You can apply these concepts to products, services, or any other ideas that you need to sell.

Pre-requisites to selling

Have a valuable product

The sales process should start with an offering that is valuable to a prospect. Only by starting with a valuable proposition – much like we did in marketing – can you have genuine confidence and belief in what you are selling. In other words, if you aren't sold on the value of what you're selling, you will struggle to persuade anyone to part with his or her cash. So be sure to always start with something that you know will benefit others.

Maintain a positive attitude

Positive emotions are contagious. If you sell with passion and enthusiasm it will rub off on other people and they will be more likely to side with you. However, if you are miserable that too can be contagious. And since a negative state puts people on the defensive and narrows their thinking,[3] they will struggle to see the possibilities of what you have to offer. For these reasons it pays to stay positive. The following *Tip* box offers a few pointers on how you can achieve this.

☑ Tip: How to stay positive in sales

When trying to sell something be prepared to hear 'no' more often than 'yes'. A salesperson might have to speak to 100 people just to make ten sales. But to succeed you have to learn to stay buoyant in an ocean of rejection.[4] How can you achieve this? Here are three quick tips to help:

- **Don't take 'no' personally**; it rarely ever is personal (also see Chapter 5 on how to respond to setbacks).
- **Have an abundance mindset**; there are lots of people out there who could be your customers. And remember, every *no* gets you closer to a *yes*!
- **For every 'no' you get, find three things to cheer you up.** Research shows that people who have a 3:1 ratio of positive feelings to negative feelings lead happier lives.[5] So if you get a 'no', find something to laugh about, call a friend to catch up, or simply count your blessings. If you can find something to lift your spirits you'll quickly bounce back from setbacks.

Plan ahead

This sounds obvious but it's easy to overlook how much you need to prepare. Therefore, before you try to sell anything make sure you know your product or service inside out. Nothing is more off-putting than a salesperson who doesn't know what they are talking about. So before you get started, be sure to brush up on the following:

- Be up to date on general industry knowledge.
- Know your competitors' strengths and weaknesses (but don't bad mouth them).
- Understand your target customers' needs, worries, and aspirations.
- Be clear about the benefits of your product or service (more on this later).

Let's now look at how you can engage a sales process effectively.

Principles of selling

Ask lots of questions

Selling is partially a discovery process. You need to learn about your prospects before you can sell them anything. This helps you discover whether your business is a good fit for a prospect or not. And the best way to kick-start such a process is through questions.

Incidentally, using questions means that when you are selling you should be doing more listening than talking. It is usually amateur salespeople who talk so much that they talk themselves out of a sale. You should aim to do the opposite. Talk less. Listen more.

What makes a good set of questions? There are a few rules of thumb you can follow (more on that below) but if you understand why questions matter you won't have to memorise these rules. Here are the key reasons to keep in mind:

- Questions help you 'qualify' whether the person you are talking to is likely to be a customer. One conversation might go as follows…

> **Salesperson offering dog-walking services**
>
> **Salesperson:** 'When's the last time you had to walk your dog?'
>
> Notice that this question is better than saying something like 'are you interested in purchasing my dog-walking services?'
>
> **Prospect:** 'Oh, my parents look after my dog now.'

The salesperson has identified that this prospect does not need a dog-walking service. The salesperson can politely move on to another prospect.

However, also notice that an astute salesperson might then refocus his or her questions to learn more about the parents of the prospect. Could the business help free up the prospect's parents so they can have time for other activities? The salesperson would need to ask more questions.

- Questions help the customer uncover needs they may not be aware they have. For example...

Salesperson runs a tutoring business

Salesperson: 'Ever thought about getting a tutor for your studies?'

Prospect: 'No, I do all studying and revision on my own.'

Salesperson: 'I used to as well. Sometimes it was manageable but when things got hectic it became a handful. Tell me, how much of a headache is it trying to revise for exams while also getting your dissertation and all other coursework done?'

Prospect: 'Actually, now that I've thought about it, that can be frustrating! We have so much coursework we rarely have time to plan for exams properly.'

Salesperson: 'Those are exactly the type of situations where we can help. Here are some strategies our clients have used. Maybe our service can be of use to you...'

Notice how the sales person used a simple question – 'how much of a headache is it to do such and such...' – to gauge and uncover a customer problem. These are the techniques great salespeople use time and time again.

- Questions can also help you discover any concerns or objections the prospect may have about what you are selling. It's always better to deal with these objections early rather than have a customer walk away with buyer's remorse.

How can you generate good questions? Sales expert Bob Etherington offers one framework that can help.[6] In Figure 10.1 we will use an example of a graphics designer attempting to sell their services to a hairdresser. Try to reflect on why these questions are better than regular statements about a product or service.

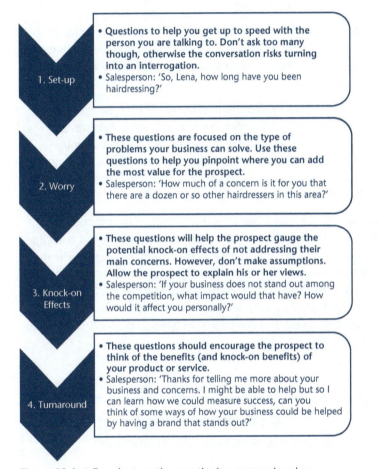

1. Set-up
- Questions to help you get up to speed with the person you are talking to. Don't ask too many though, otherwise the conversation risks turning into an interrogation.
- Salesperson: 'So, Lena, how long have you been hairdressing?'

2. Worry
- These questions are focused on the type of problems your business can solve. Use these questions to help you pinpoint where you can add the most value for the prospect.
- Salesperson: 'How much of a concern is it for you that there are a dozen or so other hairdressers in this area?'

3. Knock-on Effects
- These questions will help the prospect gauge the potential knock-on effects of not addressing their main concerns. However, don't make assumptions. Allow the prospect to explain his or her views.
- Salesperson: 'If your business does not stand out among the competition, what impact would that have? How would it affect you personally?'

4. Turnaround
- These questions should encourage the prospect to think of the benefits (and knock-on benefits) of your product or service.
- Salesperson: 'Thanks for telling me more about your business and concerns. I might be able to help but so I can learn how we could measure success, can you think of some ways of how your business could be helped by having a brand that stands out?'

Figure 10.1: A flowchart on the questioning process in sales

Sell benefits not features

Which of these statements do you find more persuasive:

- 'You will love this mobile phone. It has a quad-core chip, 2 GB of RAM, and a 3,000mAh battery. You won't find these high-spec features elsewhere.'

Chapter 10

- 'This phone uses less power, so you get a longer battery life and you can browse the Internet and talk to friends for longer. Not only that but it has a chip that makes webpages load twice as fast. You won't have to worry about those awkward times when you try to show a funny video to a friend only for the clip to take so long to load that it kills the moment.'

Great salespeople do more of the latter. The first option is a series of lifeless features that don't mean much to most people. In contrast, the second option explains the advantages of the features and makes a sale more persuasive.

In light of the above, it's important to know the difference between features and advantages in order to succeed in sales. Features are the raw facts about your product or service. They won't do much in persuading other people to part with their cash. But advantages answer the 'so what question' of a feature. They help make your product or service more relevant to a prospect.

You can also go beyond advantages by helping your prospect identify the 'benefits' of your product or service. That is, out of all the advantages your product or service offers, which of them are the most relevant to a prospect? If you can identify these 'benefits' you will be more likely to succeed in sales. And if the prospect can discover and identify these benefits themselves (with some prompting from your questions), they won't feel like they have been *sold*. They will feel like they have *bought*.

Chapter 10

⌘ Entrepreneur's Insight
Ben Grech, co-founder of Uniplaces.com

One of the first business opportunities Ben spotted occurred when he was in sixth form. The school staff had just outlawed an annual student boat party after complaints from the locals, but instead of being disappointed Ben saw a good business opportunity. If the school was not going to arrange the event, Ben would organise it himself. The venture ultimately worked out well and Ben came away with a lesson about sales that he'll never forget:

*It was actually the first marketing lesson that I learnt. That was
actually a really interesting and a very vivid lesson that still applies
now. Which is, when I put the posters up the first thing I did was to
do a picture of the boat. So I had a picture of the boat on the posters
and surprisingly no one was interested in seeing a picture of a boat
on the River Thames. And actually I had a business studies teacher
at the time who I used to talk to a lot because I was really interested
in all this stuff. And he was like, 'let me see the posters' and he
looked at them and was like, 'What's this? You've got a picture of a
boat? People don't want to go and see a boat, they want to party.
They want to have a crazy night out.' So I was like okay. I changed
the picture to like a club scene with lights and stuff. And it's the
whole thing about selling the experience and not the product. Selling
the benefits and not the product...*

*And when I started putting those posters up and started selling it
more in that way – like rather than 'I'm doing a boat party', I was
like 'You're gonna have an amazing crazy night that you've always
wanted' – then everyone became interested in it... I sold like
200 tickets, pretty much like one-to-one for £20 each!*

Chapter 10

Manage objections

We all have a natural resistance to being sold. If we weren't so
sceptical we'd probably all go bankrupt from buying everything that
was sold to us.[7] So when people resist your sales approach, don't take
it personally. However, to avoid being rattled by objections you need
to know what to expect. Here are four types of common objections
you will need to be familiar with:[8]

- The price is too high.
- The product or service won't work as promised.
- The product or service seems too difficult to use.
- There is no current need for your offering.

Regardless of what kind of business you set up, you must be prepared
to deal with most, if not all, of these objections. Here's how you can
manage each one.

- 'Price' – Emphasise the benefits of your product or service and the value it can generate for your customer or the worries it can eliminate. For example, if you are a personal trainer and your prospect raises the issue of price, try using these questions:

> - What would a great body and mind be worth to you?
> - What sort of things could you accomplish if you felt more energised on a daily basis?
> - In what ways would a sharper mind contribute to your goals?

- 'It won't work' or 'it's too difficult to use' – You can share success stories of other people who have benefited from your service. This should give the prospect more confidence. You can also use education-based selling. This is where you help your prospect become more informed.[9] Such a process could involve creating social media content (blog posts and podcasts) that explain how your product or service works.

- 'No current need' or 'it can wait' – Sometimes the prospect will not have a current need for your product or service. In this instance, you can move on to another prospect. However, if you feel that there are certain 'knock-on effects' you haven't uncovered, try digging further with questions to help your prospect identify hidden issues.

 Food for Thought

Think back to the concepts we identified in Chapter 5. We learnt that planning ahead can prevent you from being rattled by challenges. But apart from preparing for objections, are there any other endurance concepts we can apply to the sales process?

Build rapport

The final principle to consider is that customers prefer to buy from people they like. And for salespeople to be liked they need to be good listeners; they need to understand a customer's preferences; and they should share things in common with their prospects. Without these qualities it can be difficult to establish rapport and this makes selling more difficult.

However, if you can listen well and demonstrate empathy, you are more likely to get along with your prospect. It also helps if you can demonstrate things you share in common with your target customers. This could be anything from music tastes, football teams, TV shows, or hobbies.

With that said, does likeability mean that we also have to be extroverts and the 'life of a party'? Not necessarily. Research shows that extroverts are not that much better at selling than introverts.[10] In fact, the best balance is somewhere in the middle. You need to be extroverted enough to initiate the conversation but introverted enough to be thoughtful and considerate of others.[11]

Chapter summary

- Selling is the process of turning prospects into customers.
- Selling can also be defined more generally as the process of persuading others to part with their resources (attention, time, cash) in exchange for what you have to offer.
- It's important to learn how to sell because in a new venture you have to persuade people to buy your products, services, and business story.
- Before you sell anything make sure your business has a valuable product and that you are well prepared. It also helps to maintain a positive attitude throughout the process.
- To be a better salesperson you need to (1) use lots of questions, (2) sell benefits not features, (3) manage objections, and (4) build rapport with your prospects.

Chapter 10

📖 Reflection

You can prepare for a sales pitch by using Table 10.1 below. First, list the *features* of your product or service. Then, list the *advantages* of these features. After that, make a list of all the possible *benefits* your product could provide to a customer. By learning this table you will better prepared for any sales opportunity you may come across.

The first example below uses a social media marketing business. Feel free to note down some ideas of your own.

Table 10.1: Feature–advantage–benefit analysis

Features	Advantages	Possible Benefits
We create content for your website (blog posts, videos, tweets). We can produce this content in 3–5 days and to your specification.	Blog posts, videos, and tweets will attract people to your website more effectively than any other means of marketing.	If customers see your social media efforts they are more likely to engage with your brand. This will translate into more sales and ultimately more cash for you.

Useful resources

- Book: *Selling Skills for Complete Amateurs* (2008) by Bob Etherington

  Why is it worth reading?
  It's a great introduction to selling, with lots of practical techniques you can apply immediately to any sales process.

- Book: *To Sell is Human: The Surprising Truth About Persuading, Convincing, and Influencing Others* (2014) by Daniel Pink

  Why is it worth reading?
  This book takes a very modern approach and shares interesting insights on the nature of selling and persuasion. If you are interested in psychology you will like it!

- Movie: *Glengarry Glen Ross* (1992) starring Al Pacino, Kevin Spacey, and Alec Baldwin

  Why is it worth watching?
  This drama is based on the lives of four salesmen who have one week to make enough sales in order to keep their jobs. The movie has a stellar cast and is a must-watch if you are a movie buff.

Branding

What you will gain from this chapter:

1. A first step in learning about brands by focusing on names.
2. Learn about the process of naming businesses.
3. Be able to generate name ideas for your ventures.

Why names matter in branding

Branding starts with a name and names serve one main purpose: unique identification. In 11th century England this process couldn't have been any simpler. There was no need for surnames since village populations were small and people could be identified by just one name.[1] However, this all changed when populations grew.

To identify someone, people started to use a more distinctive process that gave way to the surnames we know today. For example, one method that grew popular was to combine a first name with someone's profession: a *tailor* named John became 'John the tailor', and ultimately John Taylor. Another method was to use a birthplace e.g. Mary from Berkley (which evolved into Mary Berkley). Other personal characteristics could also be used: 'Brian the strong-armed fella' morphed into Brian Armstrong.

Today people can be uniquely identified with surnames and behind each family name there is history and meaning. The same could also be said of business names. Thousands of new businesses are created every day and with a growing population, it's important to not only come up with a name that's unique but also one that is memorable and expressive. These three factors – uniqueness, memorability, and expressiveness – are crucial to creating a great brand name and they will be the focus of this chapter. But first, let us review a few naming basics.

 Food for Thought

What are your favourite brands? What's good about their names? Are they unique, memorable, and expressive?

Naming basics

Time

Don't spend forever trying to come up with a name for your business. The name you come up with matters, but only to the extent that it is legal and doesn't offend people or misrepresent what your business stands for.

Put another way, it's not the name that makes the business. The business makes the name. Brands like *Nike, Apple,* and *Disney* all have an air of brilliance mainly because they are incredibly successful organisations (they also have large advertising budgets). However, if *Nike* made poor sports shoes, the fact that its name comes from the Greek goddess of victory would have no bearing on how well the business performed.

A good name *does* count, but not as much as a good business model. So instead of spending hundreds of hours trying to come up with a perfect name, you're better off spending a few days on the exercise and focusing the rest of your time on building a fantastic business.

Research

Whatever name you come up with for your business, be prepared to run an exhaustive search to make sure it is not illegal or offensive. In the UK, for example, it is illegal to use a name that's already taken. It's also illegal to use a name that sounds very similar to another business. Furthermore, if you live in England watch out for words like 'British', 'Queen', and 'Police'. They are considered sensitive and can't be used in a business name without approval from the Secretary of State.

Aside from the obvious legal requirements it also helps to research language and cultural differences. Examples of blunders in this area include *Irish Mist*, an alcoholic beverage that struggled to do well in Germany because 'mist' means 'manure' in German. Another example is *Super-Piss*, a Finnish anti-freeze product that would no doubt struggle to be taken seriously in the UK.

Flexibility

Coming up with a business name can be a fun process (more on this in the following *Tip* box) but don't put too much pressure on yourself to come up with something amazing right away. Names *do* change and evolve with time. For example, *Yahoo* was originally called *David and Jerry's Guide to the World Wide Web*. However, within a few months of launching the business the founders changed the name to something shorter but arguably just as amusing – *Yahoo*! (with the exclamation mark).

So feel free to be creative and work hard at generating good ideas but don't expect perfection right away. Simply create a list of five to ten or more names and use the devices in the next section to help shape your name ideas into something that can have impact.

Chapter 11

☑ Tip: Five ways to generate name ideas

Struggling to come up with a name for your business? Try the following hacks in Table 11.1 to get your creative juices flowing.

Table 11.1: How to generate name ideas

Hack	Examples
Misspellings – Take any word and make it unique by misspelling it on purpose.	*Google* is a misspelt version of the number googol (which is 1 followed by 100 zeros). *Reebok* is a different spelling of the rhebok antelope.
Abbreviations – Take long words or phrases and shorten them by keeping just the key words or letters.	*BMW* is an abbreviation of *Bayerische Motoren Werke*. *Lego* is short for the Danish words 'leg godt', which mean 'play well'.
Compounds – Combine different words to make new words or phrases.	*Instagram* is a combination of the words 'instant' and 'telegram'. *YouTube* combines the pronoun 'you' with the word 'tube' (a play on retro televisions which had cathode ray tubes).
Nouns – Use a name of a distinctive thing, person, or place.	*Nando's* was named after its founder, Fernando Duarte. *Starbucks* got its name from Mr Starbuck, a character in the novel *Moby Dick*.
Foreign or ancient languages – Translate a word from one language into another.	*Audi* was named after its founder August Horch. ('Hoch' in German roughly translates to 'listen' in English, and 'listen' in Latin is 'audi'.)

The naming toolbox

One way of ranking name ideas is to use the four factors described in this section. That is, you can rank name ideas according to differentiation, expressiveness, expansiveness, and memorability. We consider each in turn below.

Differentiated

Why does the computer name *Apple* stand out? The clue lies in the names of its early competitors: *Radio Shack TRS-80*, *Atari 800*, *Commodore 64*, and *Commodore VIC-20*. In the 1970s such names were commonplace for personal computers. But here's the thing, the names were inorganic, cold, and technical. It was only *Apple* that chose something 'fruity'. Their ethos – 'think different' – did not just apply to the type of machines they manufactured. It also applied to their branding, which had a contrasting effect when compared to their competitors and the cold world of machines.

If the purpose of a name is unique identification, then it's important to choose a name that clearly differentiates you from the rest of the pack. For instance, if your dream business is a bakery but all your competitors have names with the words 'bakery' or 'cakes' (e.g. *Brandy's Bakery*, *Hot Cakes Bakery*) differentiation could be achieved by going for something that does not use similar words. Instead, you could choose names like *The Sponge Room* or *Oriel's Oven*. When it comes to branding and business names, think different!

Expressive

A good name is expressive. At the one extreme it can merely describe what your business does (e.g. the computer games manufacturer *EA* has a name that's simply an abbreviation of *Electronic Arts*). On the other extreme, a name can be more implicit and merely hint at your philosophy (e.g. the laptop manufacturer *Acer* got its name from the Latin word for 'sharpness'). Whatever the name, try to imbue within it the function or personality of your business.

Expansive

Your business could launch doing one thing but later on pivot to other products and services. Therefore, it's worth considering names that are expansive. That is, names that will grow with you as you develop your business. The mobile phone maker *Nokia*, for example, was originally a Finnish paper mill business. But had they limited their identity to something like *Fredrik's Paper Mill Company* they would have had to rebrand in order to accommodate new products.

Something similar happened with the cosmetics manufacturer *Avon*, who were originally called *The California Perfume Company*. It wasn't until the founder, David McConnell, travelled to England that he decided to rename the business after the English town Stratford-on-Avon. Indeed, the new name, *Avon*, freed the business to associate the brand with products beyond perfumes. So do keep flexibility in mind when choosing a name for your own venture.

> ☑ **Tip: When to change a name**
>
> It's OK to change your business name so long as you do it early and cheaply. It would be extremely expensive for *Nokia* and *Avon* to change their business names now because they have already built up their brands and that's what people know them as. So if you start with a name you are not sure about, aim to make amendments before your business takes off.

Memorable

Your business name has to be memorable, otherwise you will struggle to attract and retain interest in your venture. Fortunately there are several routes to memorability so let's consider a few that you can use right away.

First, one of the easiest ways of contributing to memorability is to have a short business name. Here's a rule of thumb that can help: have a name that's three syllables or less. Some of the snappiest names follow this rule: *Pizza Hut* is three syllables long. *Pepsi* is two syllables short. And *Gap* has just one syllable. Follow the rule of 'three syllables or less' and no doubt you'll have a name that's easier to remember.

Second, choose names that are simple, easy to spell, and easy to pronounce. Such names require less brainpower to recall. Research shows that people find such names to be more familiar and likeable. Not only that but some people expect companies with simple names to do better than companies with difficult names. This effect was highlighted in research carried out by psychologists Daniel Oppenheimer and Adam Alter. In the study, the researchers found that companies with simple names debuted on the stock market with better share prices than companies with complicated names.[2] Simply put, when it comes to first impressions investors are more likely to be drawn to a company with a name like *Dell* rather than a business with a name like *Boehringer Ingelheim*. So aim for simplicity and you'll already have a head start.

Finally, you can use poetic devices to achieve memorability. Some of the favourites include:

1. Alliteration – using the same sound or consonant at the beginning of each word, e.g. <u>D</u>unkin' <u>D</u>onuts
2. Assonance – using the same vowels within each word, e.g. *The R<u>o</u>lling St<u>o</u>nes*, or *V<u>o</u>da-f<u>o</u>ne*)
3. Rhyme – using the same sound at the end of each word, e.g. *7-Eleven*

Coca-Cola is perhaps the best example of poetic devices used in combination for a powerful effect. In fact, the name uses all three devices mentioned above. In the words *Coca Cola* the first letter of each word is a 'c' (alliteration); both words have an 'o' within them (assonance); and each word ends with the same sound, the vowel 'a' (rhyme).

In sum, if you can't keep a name short and simple, poetic devices can be a great help. Failing that, you can always go to the other extreme with something long but catchy, such as the brand *I Can't Believe It's Not Butter!*

 Food for Thought

Great names generate good first impressions. But after that your business must also demonstrate substance. In the study mentioned earlier (by researchers Daniel Oppenheimer and Adam Alter), companies with complicated names performed worse than organisations with simpler names on their stock market debut. However, this effect didn't last. The simplicity of a name could only be used to predict share-price performance in the short-term. After six months a company name was a poor predictor of share price performance. So yes, a good name attracts interest but once people have more information about the quality of your business, the name won't matter as much.

Chapter summary

- Branding starts with a good business name so it's important to have a label that stands out.
- If you are struggling with name ideas, try creative abbreviations, quirky spellings, unique combinations of words or nouns, or foreign language translations.
- You can shortlist business names by ranking them according to how differentiated, expressive, expansive, and memorable they are.
- But note, in the long-term business names are not as important as the quality of your business idea. So don't spend too long pondering names.
- As long as you cover the bases highlighted in this chapter you don't need to spend that much more time (or money) on the naming process.

📖 Reflection

Do you have names in mind for your business but can't figure out which one to pick? Try using the following scorecard to rank them. Here's an example of how you can do this.

Business idea

A maths tutoring business in Bristol is trying to decide on three name ideas: (a) Maths United, (b) Abacus Tutoring, or (c) Bristol Personal Tutor. Table 11.2 provides a grade out of 5 (5 being the best) on each of the naming dimensions for all three name options.

Table 11.2: Business name scorecard

Name	Differentiated	Expressive	Expansive	Memorable	Sum
Maths United	3/5	4/5	2/5	5/5	14
Abacus Tutoring	1/5	3/5	2/5	2/5	8
Bristol Personal Tutor	0/5	1/5	3/5	2/5	6

Useful resources

- Book: *Brand Against the Machine: How to Build Your Brand, Cut Through the Marketing Noise, and Stand Out from the Competition* (2011) by John Michael Morgan

  Why is it worth reading?
  Branding has many branches of knowledge. Nonetheless, this book will give you good coverage. It provides actionable steps that go beyond just naming your business and offers a framework you can use to build a brand that will stand out against the noise.

Finance

What you will gain from this chapter:

1. Understand why basic finance knowledge matters.
2. Learn about the 'Profit & Loss' and 'Balance Sheet' statements.
3. Acquire basic knowledge on how to manage cash.

Knowing your numbers

Sir Richard Branson was once given a set of financial statements to review at a board meeting. However, he struggled to make sense of the numbers and that's when a colleague realised something: their boss did not know the difference between 'net' and 'gross'.

Bear in mind that Branson is dyslexic. He struggled academically at school[1] but did not let it get in the way of him becoming a successful entrepreneur. Perhaps it was the humility of enlisting the help of others to complement his strengths that got him ahead. Nonetheless, this is exactly what Branson did at the board meeting. He owned up that he did not understand 'net' and 'gross' and a colleague offered to explain the terms using an analogy similar to the following:

> Imagine a sea with lots of fish, that's your turnover. Then imagine throwing a net into that sea and capturing some of

the fish; that's your gross profit. Then finally, imagine that as you pull the net out of the sea, some of the fish escape. Whatever you're left with in the net is your 'net profit'. [2] 🎵🎵

Before the explanation Branson had the concepts of 'net' and 'gross' mixed up. He thought that his company's gross figure was the net profit and that the business was doing better than it really was. But after he grasped the concepts Branson had a more accurate picture of his business and could make more informed decisions.

What's the moral of the story? If you don't understand basic financial concepts you won't know how well your business is really doing. So regardless of whether you like numbers or not, it's helpful to develop some basic financial literacy during your entrepreneurial journey.

With that being said, Branson takes the view that knowing all the financial lingo doesn't matter as much. Sure, you need to be able to do basic arithmetic. But Branson suggests that you can always hire an accountant for the complicated work. [3] Alternatively, you could partner up with someone who is more of a numbers person than you are. In either case, there's still value in knowing the basics and this chapter will walk you through them.

⌘ **Entrepreneur's Insight**
Shaleena Chanrai, co-founder of *Bella Kinesis*

Co-founding teams vary from business to business but when the co-founders of *Bella Kinesis* were asked why their partnership works well, Shaleena referred to their diversity of skill:

> *I think we make a good combination because we have such a different set of skills as well. I studied photography; I did graphic design; so I can do the creative side of things. I did all of our branding [though] I'm not very good with numbers, but she [the co-founder] is. And what's great is that we sort of teach each other, because if I don't understand the financials, I get stuck. If I'm out of town and she doesn't know how to resize an image, then again, she's stuck. So I think it works because we have a different set of skills but we're also teaching each other because right now it is just the two of us.*

☑ **Tip: Managing cash**

Cash is the lifeblood of business; running out of cash is the most elemental reason why companies go bust. As such, it is important to keep a close eye on your business cash balance and to manage it with care. Below is a list of some ideas that will help you with cash management:

- **Collecting Cash** – Whenever you make a sale, try to collect the cash as soon as possible. If you sell to consumers this shouldn't be a problem since payment is often immediate. However, if you are supplying to businesses, negotiate payment terms where you can be paid within a few days rather than waiting for 30–60 days (this is the most common payment period in business-to-business selling).

- **Paying Suppliers** – The flipside to collecting cash early is delaying payments by a reasonable and acceptable amount of time. When you are a new business, some suppliers will demand that you pay for goods or services the moment they are delivered. However, try to negotiate payment terms of 14 days or more to give you some wiggle room.

- **Frugal Mentality** – At the start-up stage of a business, keep an eye on cash every day. Be critical about every expenditure because you will need as much cash as possible to give you time to develop and grow your business. In sum, the more cash you have the longer you have to try to make your business a success!

Profit and loss

One of the most important words in business is profit (the most consequential is actually 'cash', but we've already covered that in the previous *Tip* box). And a lot can go into calculating this figure.

For a large business the profit figure is often different from the cash that ends up in the bank. One reason for this is that in accounting it's possible to recognise some costs against your profit even if no money has left the bank (e.g. accountants recognise the ageing of an asset as a regular deduction against revenues even though there's no actual cash paid). In contrast, the accounts of a young and small business are simpler. Therefore, our focus here is on the basic version of profit, the essence of which is this:

- If you make more money than you've spent, you're in profit.
- If you make less money than what you have spent, then you're at a loss.
- And so profit (or loss) is calculated as income minus expenses.

> **Key term – Profit Calculation:**
> Profit = Income – Expenses

Why it matters

A profit figure is useful because it tells us how well a business has performed over a certain period of time. Accounts that are published for public scrutiny usually report on a twelve-month period but within a business, performance and profit figures are monitored monthly, weekly, or even daily.

When you hear the word 'profit' you'll also often hear other words like gross, net, cost of goods, overheads, margins, and so on. All these terms are cousins to the profit figure and also provide information on how well the business is doing. They can also be used to diagnose specific areas of weakness in a venture. To put these terms into perspective, a simple profit and loss (or income) statement of a fictional smoothie business is provided in Table 12.1.

Table 12.1: Income statement sample

Income Statement	£	Comment
Revenue	1,000	**Revenue** is the total amount of money you make from your customers. Some people call it 'sales' or 'income'. _Calculation:_ • Sold 500 smoothies for £2 each.
Cost of Goods **Empty bottles** **Juice** **Wages**	(50) (125) (500)	**Cost of Goods** is how much it costs to make the products you sold. Some people call it 'cost of sales'. Usually the more you sell, the higher this figure will be. It's a 'variable cost'.

Chapter 12

Table 12.1: (continued)

Income Statement	£	Comment
Gross Profit	325	**Gross Profit** is how much you have left when you deduct your 'direct' costs from your revenue.
Gross Profit Margin	33%	**Gross Margin** is the percentage of sales that represent your gross profit. *Calculation:* Gross Margin = (Gross Profit ÷ Revenue) x 100
Operating Costs **Stall hire** **Facebook advert** **Flyers** **Travel costs** **Stationery**	 (25) (40) (15) (30) (15)	**Operating Costs** are any other costs incurred while running a business. Because these costs can't be linked directly to any one product sold, they are also called 'overheads'. They support the whole business and are usually 'fixed' regardless of the number of products sold.
Net Profit	200	**Net Profit** is how much you're left with after deducting all your costs.
Net Profit Margin	20%	**Net Margin** is the percentage of sales that represent your net profit. Some people also call it 'profit margin' (though this is a bit ambiguous and doesn't say whether it's gross or net margin). *Calculation:* Net Margin = (Net Profit ÷ Revenue) x 100

☑ **Tip: Improving financial performance**

An income statement is a good place to start if you wish to improve the profits of your business. To grow profits you can either work on your revenue, costs, or both.

Growing revenue

Here are four ways you can grow your revenue:[4]

- Get more customers.
- Entice customers to buy larger quantities.

- Persuade customers to buy more frequently.
- Increase your prices (but do so with caution since people may simply switch to a lower-cost competitor).

Cutting costs

Costs are a necessary part of business. But that doesn't mean we can't be smarter about how we spend money. Here are some tips you can use in your venture:

- Are you getting supplies at the best prices? Make sure you do by negotiating or researching other suppliers.
- Do you really need those fancy business cards? Spend cash only on what matters!
- Do you really need to employ someone? Try doing the work yourself and only hire if you are completely stretched for time.

Balance sheet

In business, a balance sheet summarises what a company owns and what it owes. At the outset of starting a new venture you are unlikely to encounter this financial statement but as a new entrepreneur it helps to know the basics. This involves knowing the difference between assets, liabilities, equity, and capital – the building blocks of a 'balance sheet'. What exactly is this mysterious device about?

A balance sheet is like a weighing scale. On one side you have assets (i.e. everything a business owns) and on the other you have liabilities and equity (i.e. everything a business owes to you or other people). In practice, both sides are always equal since it's impossible for a business to own things that are worth more than the combination of what's due back to investors and other people. And so the balance sheet, if prepared correctly, always 'balances' (see Figure 12.1).

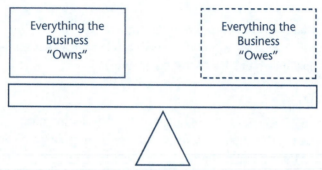

Figure 12.1: Balance sheet concept

Where do assets, liabilities, and equity fall on the weighing scale? We can adjust Figure 12.1 to show these components in Figure 12.2.

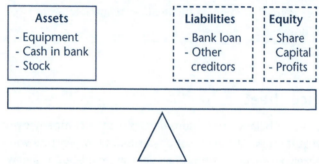

Figure 12.2: Detailed balance sheet items

Assets

The left side of the scale represents assets. These are the resources that the business owns. They include property, equipment, and stock or inventory. Assets generate value for a business.

Liabilities and equity

The right hand of the scale includes what the business owes to other people. This group includes liabilities and equity. Liabilities are essentially debt. Loans, overdrafts, and amounts owed to suppliers all fall into this category. Equity is rather different. It mainly represents two things: what the owner has invested in the business ('share capital' or 'start-up capital') and profits retained by the business.

In general, the right hand side of our scale summarises how the business is funded. That is, you can either start a company with other people's money (debt), your own funds (capital), or a mix of both.

Why it matters

You won't have to worry too much about a balance sheet at the outset of a new business. However, a related idea that's important to keep in mind is this: a healthy business should have more assets than liabilities. This is because having large debts (liabilities) increases the risk of 'bankrupting' your venture through interest costs that eat away at profits and cash balances.

If all of this seems a bit foreign at the moment don't be alarmed. Knowing the basics is absolutely fine when you are starting out. To see what a balance sheet looks like, see Table 12.2.

Table 12.2: Balance sheet sample

Balance Sheet	£	Comment
<u>Assets</u>	–	**Assets** are resources the business owns. Here we have a very expensive blender, a bit of cash, and a computer. All these items help the business to make money.
Blender	500	
Cash	1,000	
Computer	500	
TOTAL ASSETS	**2,000**	
<u>Current Liabilities</u>	–	**Liabilities** are the amounts owed to other people. They are usually split between 'current liabilities' (amounts due within a year) and long-term debts.
Money owed to farmer	(100)	
<u>Long-term Liabilities</u>		
Bank loan	(500)	
TOTAL LIABILITIES	**(600)**	
<u>Equity</u>	–	**Equity** is what's owed to the owners of the business. In this example the owners invested £1,200 in total. The company also owes them £200 of profits from the year.
Share Capital	(1,200)	
Retained Profit	(200)	
TOTAL EQUITY	**1,400**	
LIABILITIES+EQUITY	**2,000**	When you add up what the business owes to other people (liabilities) as well as what it owes to the owners (equity), the sum should be equal to all the resources (assets) the business has.

Chapter 12

☑ **Tip: Raising money for your venture**

Where to find cash

Cash can be hard to come by when you're a graduate, especially when you have a student loan, bills, and rent to pay. Even so, it's best to start with your own savings to first prove that your business can make money before you risk other people's funds. Alternatively Table 12.3 has a few examples of sources of finance you may consider.

Table 12.3: Types of finance

Type	Pros	Cons	Examples of Options
Debt finance	You keep 100 percent of your business.	You have to pay interest on the loan and depending on the lender, you may be personally liable if the company can't pay back the debt.	Visit these websites to learn about some of the options available to UK entrepreneurs: *www.startuploans.co.uk* *www.virginstartup.org*
Equity investment	There's no interest to pay.	You have to give up some control of your business. Also, it's difficult to get unless your business is already making money.	Crowdfunding options: *www.seedrs.com* *www.crowdcube.com* (Note: alternative crowdfunder that doesn't take shares in your business is www.kickstarter.com)
Grant	Effectively free money but with conditions attached to how the cash is used.	They are very difficult to get and may not be available for your type of business.	Visit the following link and filter by grants: *https://www.gov. uk/business-finance-support-finder/search*

How much to raise

Every business is different and there are no hard rules on how much money you need to start. However, a general rule of thumb is to have enough cash to keep you going for at least 18 months. (Remember in Chapter 5 we learnt that it can take around 6–12 months of trade to gauge whether a business idea is reasonable.)

Putting it all together

With all sorts of financial information to consider, what should your priorities be when you start a new business? One way to think about the key financial metrics is through a hierarchy of priorities.

You may already be familiar with Maslow's hierarchy of needs, where Maslow proposed the following: humans need to have their very basic needs met first (food, water, safety) before they can fulfil higher aims (love, social status, personal growth). The same idea can apply to your venture. Basic needs have to be met first before you can direct efforts to higher aims. Figure 12.3 offers one way of understanding this concept.

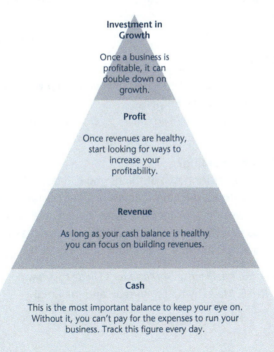

Figure 12.3: Financial priorities

Chapter summary

- Financial metrics help us understand the performance and health of a business.
- Profits are what you have left over when you deduct expenses from income.
- It's possible to improve profits by getting customers to spend more and by managing your costs.
- The financial health of a business can also be determined by reviewing its balance sheet.
- A balance sheet shows what the business owns (assets) and what it owes its owners (equity) and other people (liabilities).
- Healthy businesses have more assets than liabilities.
- When you start a business, always keep an eye on your cash balance. Cash is the lifeblood of business and without it a company can't function.
- If finance and accounting gives you a headache, try to learn just the basics and team up with someone else who can take a lead on the numbers.

Useful resources

- Blog: *5 Clever Ways to Raise Money for Your Startup Without Making an Investor Pitch* by Dave Kerpen
  http://www.inc.com/dave-kerpen/5-clever-ways-to-raise-money-for-your-startup-without-making-an-investor-pitch.html

  Why is it worth reading?
  The article is a brief rundown of things you can do to fund your venture without pitching to investors. (Remember, most professional investors look for businesses that are already making money. So as you start out, consider alternative avenues such as those in this article in order to get your business off the ground.)

- Book: *Financial Intelligence: A Manager's Guide to Knowing What the Numbers Really Mean* by Karen Berman and Joe Knight

Why is it worth reading?
If you decide to be the numbers person in your venture then this book is a must-read. It is largely jargon-free and explains profit and loss, the balance sheet, and cash concepts in a lot more detail. Also, the business magazine *Inc* rates this book as the best and clearest guide to the financial literacy.

Process

In Part 2 of the book we explored some of the fundamental skills of entrepreneurship. We looked at strategy, marketing, sales, branding, and the basics of finance and accounting. These are skills that you will continue to develop during your entrepreneurial journey, but now we must turn to matters of action.

In Part 3 we will explore the entrepreneurial process first identified in Chapter 2. More specifically, we will look at how you can identify, evaluate, and exploit business opportunities.

Identifying opportunities

What you will gain from this chapter:

1. Knowledge about the nature of business ideas.
2. Be able to improve your chances of finding good ideas.
3. Learn the steps you can take to discover new business opportunities.

The nature of business ideas

One of the top reasons why graduates never consider entrepreneurship is a lack of business ideas. To many, ideas are the most pivotal part of starting a business. But while there's some truth to this we should not be intimidated by the process of finding ideas. Nor should we allow this fear to deprive us of the opportunity to start a business. Once you understand the nature of business opportunities you will find that the process of discovering them is rather straightforward. This is because the core of a business idea is quite rudimental. Just think about any business venture – your favourite restaurant, retail store, or website. All these ideas originate from one of three places:

- Solving problems
- Fulfilling desires
- Creating new needs or desires to be fulfilled

These three elements can be combined or used in isolation to create new businesses. Let's look at each in turn.

To solve a problem

Businesses are primarily concerned with solving problems. Sometimes these problems are visible: for example, the taxi network company *Uber* solves the problem of getting a cab. But at other times the problems are out of sight: the online business *Joyable*, for example, is on a mission to cure the world of anxiety and depression. Regardless of industry, many businesses make money by providing solutions to real-world problems.

To fulfil a current desire

Businesses can also be created to fulfil current needs or desires. The entertainment industry is the most obvious example. When you have a desire to be entertained, you can go to the cinema, pub, or theatre.

Another example is education. This book, for instance, fulfils the desire to learn more about entrepreneurship. Notice also that this book was created to solve a problem: not knowing where to begin if you are interested in starting a business after university.

To create and fulfil a new demand

Finally, some business ideas don't solve current problems or fulfil current desires. Instead, it's possible to create a new product or service that caters to a previously unknown demand. Examples of this strategy are rare because it requires more ingenuity and is more risky, but it can also be more profitable.

For example, *Propercorn*, a snack business based in London, goes beyond the salt and sugar popcorn we're used to having. Thanks to new flavours of popcorn that include sweet coconut and vanilla, sour cream and black pepper, and Worcestershire sauce and sun-dried tomato, *Propercorn* have created demand for flavours no one had considered before. Is *Propercorn's* idea working? Sales were £6 million at the time of writing and the business is growing.

Behaviours that inspire creative ideas

Now that we know the DNA of business ideas (solving problems, fulfilling desires, creating new demand) how can we find more opportunities to start a venture? To answer this question we can refer to a study conducted by strategy and entrepreneurship experts at Harvard Business School, INSEAD, and BYU Marriott School.

In the study, the researchers set out to learn what behaviours contributed to an entrepreneur's ability to find new business ideas. They interviewed 72 entrepreneurs who between them had started 137 innovative businesses. This group included the founders of *Skype, eBay, Southwest Airlines* (the world's largest budget airline), and *Amazon*. The researchers also studied managers who were not entrepreneurs. Here's what the study found.[1]

Unlike corporate managers, entrepreneurs are good at finding unique business opportunities because they do more of the following:

1. They question things, especially the status quo.
2. They are very observant of everyday experiences and the world around them.
3. They test things often and are open to new experiences and experiments.
4. They have a diverse mix of friends and associates with whom they can bounce ideas and learn new things from.

If you can employ a combination of these behaviours you too will be able to discover more business opportunities. Let's look at how you can apply these principles in your search for a new business idea.

Questioning

What's missing from today's world? What could be done better? What convention or status quo can be disrupted? These are the types of questions successful entrepreneurs ask.

Take dating for example. The traditional way to do it is to ask someone out if you fancy them. The problem is you never know if they are interested until you talk to them. But who says you always have to risk rejection? That's the question Sean Rad asked before he created the popular dating app *Tinder*, which lets people message each other only if they have both expressed interest.

Observing

If you take time to observe what's around you – both ordinary and extraordinary encounters – you'll often find opportunities for new types of businesses. Coupled with questioning, being very observant of people and everyday occurrences can be a great way to fire up the idea discovery process.

For instance, when Howard Schultz was in Italy for a housewares trade show, he noticed something that his home country didn't have: espresso bars. These mini cafés were common in Milan but for Schultz, they were an unusual encounter. So he popped into one of the bars and discovered a unique coffee culture that brought people together in comfort. During his trip, Schultz decided to try a *caffé latte* at one of the venues and immediately knew he had to import the idea to America. The company Schultz ended up building was *Starbucks*.

Experimenting

New ideas are often found in the least likely of places. This means that it helps when you tinker and experiment with things outside your comfort zone. This may involve visiting new places (like Howard Schultz did), learning new things, trying new activities, or simply taking small, non-judgemental bets on side projects to see if an idea has legs. Without tinkering you limit the range of your ideas. (Notice also how this concept ties in with the idea of *scanning for inspiration* when attempting to be creative.)

Networks

Innovative entrepreneurs also have a habit of mixing with people from diverse backgrounds. While managers in corporate jobs may network extensively, they usually limit their social networks to people who are in the same profession or industry.

Entrepreneurs take a different approach. They know that in order to find great ideas it helps to mix things up in your social network so it isn't unusual to have doctors, artists, lawyers, and engineers in your contacts list. Such diversity opens you up to more ideas and can help you discover more business opportunities.

How to find business ideas

We've looked at the DNA of a business idea and we've also looked at the four conditions that enable entrepreneurs to discover new ideas. Putting all this together, we can now turn to concrete steps you can take to discover business ideas of your own. There are four pieces of advice to consider.

Don't try to come up with business ideas

Don't force yourself to come up with a business idea. The acclaimed investor Paul Graham equates such efforts to the equivalent of coming up with business ideas to be used in a sitcom show. This is because when you try to *come up* with business ideas, you create concepts that may sound plausible (and good enough for inclusion in a fictitious TV show about entrepreneurship) but which would not hold weight in the real world.[2]

So the first step in discovering a business idea is to *not* try to come up with ideas out of thin air. If you commit this crime you might end up with ideas like:

- Layoffspace.com – a social network for the unemployed (any thoughts on why this idea failed?)
- Yoghurt shampoo – a dairy-based shampoo product with all the natural ingredients of yoghurt (some people mistook it for food and got sick)
- iSmell – a device that added smell to internet browsing (in the end no one really wanted to smell anything while browsing the net)

Look for problems to solve

The easiest place to start if you don't have any business ideas is to observe annoyances in everyday life. For instance, Sarah Blakely invented the hosiery brand *Spanx* after she couldn't find the right hosiery to wear under white trousers.[3] Another example is Ritesh Agarwal. He started a hotel network after his frustration with the customer service of a hotel in Delhi.[4] So keep an eye out for what bugs you as this could be your next business venture.

If you come across a problem worth solving, it's also important to question its nature. More specifically, you can ask, will a solution to this problem be the equivalent of vitamins or painkillers? Vitamins are nice-to-haves. People can generally do without them. But painkillers are different. A throbbing headache will drive you to search and pay for a remedy. These are the types of problems you want to focus on since people are more willing to pay for the solutions to acute pains.[5]

Chapter 13

Finally, if a particular problem already has solutions, ask whether conventional remedies can be disrupted. What parts can you turn upside down? If the problem is too big to solve, is there a way to redefine or break it into smaller pieces? These questions will help you refine your business ideas.

Explore human needs and desires

If you can't find any problems worth solving, think about human nature. Are there certain desires and needs that are not being fulfilled well enough? If a particular need is already being met, in what ways could the status quo be disrupted?

Here are some basic human desires you can consider if you're not sure where to start.[6] (A few business examples are provided in brackets.)

- Power – a desire to influence others
- Independence – a desire for self-reliance
- Curiosity – a desire for knowledge (e.g. education services)
- Acceptance – a desire for inclusion
- Order – a desire for organisation (e.g. a cleaning or de-cluttering service business)
- Saving – a desire to collect things
- Social contact – a desire for companionship (e.g. social networks)
- Status – a desire for social standing (e.g. premium products and status symbols)
- Romance – a desire for sex and beauty (e.g. make-up products, relationship advice, counselling)
- Eating – a desire to satisfy hunger

Notice that it's possible to combine problem solving with basic human desires (e.g. *Facebook* solves the problem of staying in touch with distant friends while also fulfilling social contact and status desires).

Explore and experiment

If you can't find any problems that bug you, try observing other people. Ask them about their annoyances. Visit people that live in new places and new cities. Read about the experience of others. By exposing yourself to new stimuli, you will be able to boost your creativity and enhance your opportunity recognition skills.

⌘ **Entrepreneur's Insight**
Julien Callede, co-founder of Made.com

What makes a good business idea? This question was put to Julien Callede, co-founder of the online designer furniture retailer *Made.com*. Here's what he had to say:

I think your idea needs to make sense. You need to solve something. Either you solve a problem, or you're bringing a service or creating a product that's going to change something for people.

Chapter summary

- Finding business ideas is not as difficult as it looks if you understand the key components involved.
- Good business ideas can be reduced to one or more of the following tenets: (1) solving problems, (2) fulfilling needs or desires, and (3) creating new demand.
- If you want to be good at finding business ideas, question the status quo often, be an astute observer of the world around you, explore and experiment lots, and cultivate a diverse social network.
- When starting out, try to avoid coming up with business ideas from scratch. This is because you could end up with a plausible-sounding concept that doesn't hold any weight in reality.
- To find the best ideas look for problems worth solving. Failing that, explore basic human desires and think of ways they can be better met.

Chapter 13

Generating a list of business ideas

If you already have a business idea you can skip this section. If you don't have any ideas the following prompts will help you get started.

- **Problems** – Be observant of everyday annoyances and make a note of things that don't work so well. It could be an activity at your workplace or it could be an inconvenience at home.

- **Desires** – Pick some of the basic human desires mentioned earlier and list as many ways of fulfilling them as possible. Try combining some and see if there's anything that stands out. For example, can a desire to collect things be coupled with a desire for organisation? Maybe there's a business idea for people who love keeping all their clothes and dozens of shoes but don't have the space for it at home. Grab a pen and explore the possibilities.

Useful resources

- Book: *The $100 Startup* (2015) by Chris Guillebeau

  Why is it worth reading?
  This book will inspire you to use skills you already have to start a venture at a very low cost. The book also includes case studies of people who have turned a small venture into a six-figure operation. It's a perfect read if you'd like to try entrepreneurship without risking too much money.

Evaluating opportunities

What you will gain from this chapter:
1. Learn how to evaluate business ideas.
2. Discover one of the ways of spotting attractive industries.
3. A brief introduction to the concept of intellectual property.

Three rules of thumb

In the previous chapter we looked at a number of ways you can discover new business ideas. If you completed the exercise in that chapter you will have a list of ideas to consider. This chapter deals with the criteria you can use to select an idea to pursue. If you already have a concept you would like to explore you can also use this chapter to test how attractive the idea is.

So how do we evaluate business ideas? Business literature is filled with dozens of methods but you don't need to know all of them to proceed. Instead, here are three quick rules of thumb you can use in your assessment.

1. Industry attractiveness

One of the best ways you can improve your odds of success in entrepreneurship is by starting a business in a good industry. This strategic approach embodies the saying we came across in Chapter 8, 'a rising tide lifts all boats'. Indeed, where you choose to start a business will significantly affect how fast you'll grow and ultimately, how much money you'll make.

How important is industry choice? Data from the *Inc. 500*, an annual list of the fastest-growing private companies in the USA, reveals an astonishing fact. Between 1982 and 2002, new software businesses were 608 times more likely than restaurant start-ups to become one of the 500 fastest growing companies in America.[1] While there are regional differences in other countries, these figures highlight how important industry choice is when assessing early ideas.

To quickly check whether an industry is attractive try to work out the answers to the following three questions:

1. **Is an area growing, stagnant, or declining?** It would be hopeless to start a business in the videocassette market, for example, as the medium has since been replaced by online streaming. Almost no investor would back a business in a declining industry. But if you start a business in an area that's growing you'll find it easier to find customers and investment.

2. **Is competition limited or fierce?** Restaurant businesses, for instance, have high failure rates because of extreme competition and the ease with which ideas can be copied. The only way to overcome this obstacle is with something extremely differentiated. A niche offering (e.g. a tea-only café that offers 50 different flavours of tea) can help. Alternatively, a venture such as a gym that gives away free pizza could also be competitive; the fastest growing gym group in America at the time of writing, *Planet Fitness*, does exactly this.[2]

3. **Is the industry easy to enter?** This is a double-edged sword. If an industry is easy to enter (for example, a blog and social media content business) you will find competition fierce. On the other hand, if an industry requires a lot of cash to enter (for example, oil, gas, and energy businesses), few entrepreneurs can afford to venture into it. The sweet spot is when the barriers aren't financial but can be built up over time to defend your position. For instance, if you started a social media marketing business the way to create a barrier for others would be to establish deep relationships with advertising clients in your local area. That way if someone else was thinking of launching a business in the same area, they would learn

that even without financial barriers they still have to invest a lot of time to catch up with you in terms of client relationships.

☑ Tip: How to find attractive industries

You can check if an industry has promise by researching how much investment is going into it. This is because professional investors prefer to back companies in areas that are expected to grow. So if you 'follow the money' you can get an idea of which industries are expected to do well. To give you an idea of what this research looks like, Figure 14.1 shows data from an *Ernst and Young* report[3] that shows the spread of investments, in billions of dollars, from 2011 to 2014.

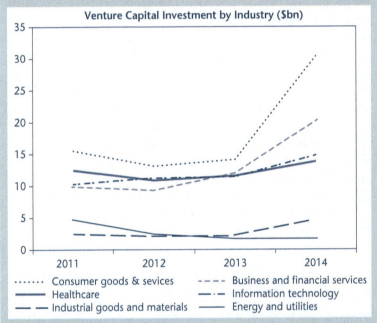

Figure 14.1: Evaluating opportunities

From the above you can see that businesses in the consumer sector are getting more investments while businesses in the energy and utilities sector are receiving less. Where would you rather be?

Note: this data is always on the move but if you google 'venture capital investments by industry' you will find up-to-date figures.

Chapter 14

2. Personal fit

The second rule of thumb you can use to pick a business idea is to reflect on personal fit. This exercise will help you evaluate the means with which you could bring your idea to fruition and whether you are fit to do so. Use the questions below to prompt your thinking. They are inspired by the work of Dr Saras Sarasvathy, a cognitive scientist who has studied entrepreneurial thinking extensively.[4]

- **Who Am I?** What am I passionate about? What would I be willing to work on for an extended period of time? Do I care enough about this idea to work on it for a minimum of 6–12 months? Do I just *like* this idea or do I *love* it? What natural talents do I have? What do people say I'm good at? Would I be happy to have this business idea as a part of my identity?
- **What do I know?** Is there knowledge from my university degree or graduate job experience that I can take advantage of? What other education experiences can I leverage? The founders of *Ben & Jerry's* ice cream knew nothing about ice cream but they took a short course on it before starting their venture. Are there any courses that you can take to improve your prospects?
- **Who do I know?** Do you have any friends, colleagues, or relatives who've worked in a business similar to the venture you have in mind? Do you know any other entrepreneurs? How about the people you went to university with? What industries are these people working in? Who in your community can you reach out to for help with this idea? Are there any diverse connections you can benefit from?

If you can generate positive answers to these questions when thinking about an idea, you are off to a good start.

3. Unique angle

It's likely that whatever your business idea, someone else has also thought about it. However, don't let this put you off. If anything, having a few competitors in a particular space legitimises the idea: it means that there's a *real* demand and that customers are willing to pay for products or services that satisfy a specific need.

What you have to weigh up though, is whether you have a unique angle that will put you ahead of the competition. You should therefore consider the answer to the following question:

● **What unique insights do I have?** What do I know that is different from what everybody else knows?[5] What edge or advantage do I bring to the table? Is there a contrarian strategy that can put me ahead? In other words, what aspect of my idea do I know will work but which few people currently appreciate or agree with?

☑ Tip: Intellectual property consideration

Before you choose an idea for your business, be sure to spend some time learning about intellectual property ('IP'). This is just a fancy word for the concept of idea ownership and the ideas involved usually relate to things like:

● Logos
● Names
● Product designs
● Software code
● Music
● Literature

All of the above can be considered intellectual property. In most countries this property is protected by patent, copyright, and trademark laws. The laws ensure that ideas are not copied without permission or reward. For example, most businesses file for the trademark protection of their name and logo. Another example is if you have a unique design for a product you can register a patent so that no one else can profit from your new invention.

Check out the resources below if you would like to learn more about the topic:

● https://www.gov.uk/intellectual-property-an-overview
● http://www.wipo.int/about-ip/en/

A final note on ideas

Finding a winning business idea is almost as unpredictable as finding the next number-one song. In retrospect great ideas seem obvious. But until you execute an idea it will be difficult to tell whether you're onto a winner. Regardless, the rules of thumb discussed above are the equivalent of singing in tune. That is, if you can sing the right notes it does not guarantee a chart-topper. However, it improves your chances of being listened to. In contrast, if you sing out of tune no one will listen. Entrepreneurship is similar. The guidelines in this chapter will help you stay 'in tune' so that you have better prospects of success. But if you ignore them you will struggle to execute a winning idea.

Chapter summary

- You can evaluate business ideas by considering (1) industry attractiveness, (2) personal fit, and (3) unique advantages.
- An industry is attractive if it's growing. But be sure to also take note of competition and barriers of entry to an industry.
- Personal fit can be assessed by considering your passions, knowledge, and industry contacts.
- Finally, try to prioritise ideas that have a unique angle. It's the only way that you will be able to stay ahead of the competition.

 Reflection

If you completed the exercise in the previous chapter, have a go at evaluating the ideas you came up with using the criteria below.

Use your judgement to assess the attractiveness of the ideas but if you are stuck, a crude assessment could involve scoring each idea on a scale of 1 to 5 (with 5 being the most attractive).

A total score of more than 10 out of 15 might be deemed attractive while anything below that could be eliminated. An example is provided in the first row of Table 14.1.

Table 14.1: Evaluating business ideas

Idea	Industry Attractiveness	Personal Fit	Unique Angle	Total Score
Food Delivery Business	5	3	1	9/15 (or 60% score) Result = Not attractive enough
My Idea				
My Idea				
My Idea				

*Use the notes section if you need more space.

Chapter 14

Useful resources

- Book: *Zero to One* (2014) by Peter Thiel (co-founder of *Paypal*) and Blake Masters

  Why is it worth reading?
  This is must-read if you are thinking of starting an app business. However, there are many lessons for ordinary entrepreneurs as well. For example, one of the themes of the book is that entrepreneurs should build something so differentiated that they create a monopoly for themselves. The book is contrarian and you won't agree with everything in it but the insights it holds are worth the debate.

Exploiting opportunities

What you will gain from this chapter:
1. Learn how to bring your idea to life.
2. Appreciate the value of having a business partner.
3. Be able to launch your venture at a low cost.

Making your idea a reality

Once you have a business idea worth pursuing, what are the next steps? There are no specific rules to follow since entrepreneurship is dynamic. Still, it's possible to create a new venture by following a number of broad strokes and in this chapter we will do exactly that.

What follows is an abridged version of the implementation stage in the entrepreneurial process.[1] And for illustrative purposes we will walk through a seven-step action plan using a fictitious business case. Example scenarios are provided in the shaded boxes but you do not need to read them all to grasp the essential concepts ahead.

Lena's grocery delivery business

Lena works in the telecoms industry as a business analyst. She graduated two years ago from the University of Manchester with a degree in English literature.

Recently Lena has become increasingly annoyed at how she gets back from work in the late hours only to find that she's run out of basic groceries. After a long day in the office she struggles to leave her city centre apartment in the late hours to buy extra milk, sugar, shampoo, or toothpaste.

Lena has wondered if there's an app business that could deliver urgent groceries to people who have busy lives like her. If such a business does not exist, she's interested in starting it. But first she may want to consider a business partner.

Step 1. Find a co-founder (or two)

Starting a business alone is tough. Fewer than 1 in 5 new ventures are founded by solo entrepreneurs in the technology sector[2] and the pattern is probably the same in other industries. Even more telling, investors rarely back companies with just one person. At *Y Combinator* – one of the world's leading investors in early-stage businesses – fewer than 10 percent of the companies they support are founded by one person.[3]

When it comes to starting a new business, the range of skills, time, and resources required are often too much for one person to bear. But if you can find a partner or two (the best number of co-founders is between 2 and 4) you can increase your odds of success.[4]

Benefits of co-founders

Having a co-founder helps in three ways. First, you'll have an extra set of hands to help out. For example if you are great at marketing but weak in accounting, having a more financially talented partner can help make your venture more rounded and effective.

Second, having a co-founder from a different background extends the social network of your business. For example, your co-founder may have friends in the press who can help you get PR. Or they might have a relative in banking who can advise you on potential avenues of funding.

Finally, having a co-founder means you don't have to go through it all alone. Entrepreneurship is very rewarding but it can also be extremely challenging. And when things get hard it can be difficult to find genuine empathy. Having a co-founder provides that extra moral support. So when you feel a bit down a good partner will encourage you. And when your partner is not feeling so good you can be there for them too.

Finding a co-founder

Lots of people start businesses with their friends. This is fine as long as you plan and account for a number of issues specific to this dynamic. For one, if you start a business with a close friend, you are less likely to benefit from the breadth of a combined social network that would come from having a business partner whose social circle doesn't overlap with yours.

Second, it can be more challenging to have difficult conversations or to disagree with friends. This is because as friends you will naturally want to protect each other's feelings. However, avoiding healthy conflict or disagreements may lead to 'groupthink', where you all agree for the sake of agreeing even when it's to the detriment of the business.

Finally, you might have a great social relationship with your friend but it's dangerous to assume that you will have a great professional relationship. Your friend might be a good listener but are they as organised as you are? You might also have common interests but are your values similar? There are countless examples of founders who have lost friends and family because of strained business relationships so it's definitely an area you should tread with caution.

Given the above, should you avoid working with friends? Not necessarily. But if you choose to do so be sure to set out ways in which you will mitigate some of the risks. For example, you might have to network more given the limits of your social mix. You might also have to push for very open debates, while making sure not to take disagreements personally. A further step you can take is to plan ahead for anything that might potentially damage your friendship, so you are clear on whether to act in the interests of the business or friendship.

If friends don't always make good co-founders where else can you look? One of the best places to start is with people you've worked with before. This could be people you did group coursework with while at university or perhaps someone you completed a project with. In both scenarios you will have a good idea of what the person is like both socially and professionally, and can therefore know what to expect when you start a business together.

⌘ **Entrepreneur's Insight**
Roshni Assomull, co-founder of Bella Kinesis

Roshni co-founded an ethical sportswear brand with her long-time friend Shaleena. They make a great team, and here's one of the reasons why:

We have this thing we established quite early on because our friendship is extremely important. We've been friends for ages so that has to survive even if the business doesn't. So we were like okay, we should have this thing once a week where we air any grievances, like 'last week you said you'd do this but you didn't'. And because sometimes it's quite difficult as friends to tell each other what to do, we decided we'd have this [open chat] once a week just to [help].

What to look for in a co-founder

The best teams in business strike a balance between homogeneity and heterogeneity. That is, you want to work with people who are somewhat similar to you but who are also different.

It is true that having things in common (e.g. values, goals, risk tolerance, levels of commitment) helps you make decisions quicker and contributes to a more harmonious working relationship. However, being too similar can also deprive you of alternatives that may be useful in other situations.

For example, if you are an introvert it's good to have a partner who's an extrovert. If you are a detail-oriented person it helps to have a big-picture co-founder. And if you are very risk-averse it can be advantageous to have someone who will inspire risk-taking in the business every now and then.

Roles and rewards

Teams work well when roles and rewards are clear. Indeed, it's better for one person to focus on the development of a product while the other is focused on selling it. And though overlaps will inevitably happen, being clear about responsibilities can keep efforts focused and consistent.

☑ Tip: Co-founder checklist

☐ Have you worked with your potential co-founder before?
☐ Do they have a different background and different set of skills from you?
☐ Are roles, responsibilities, and rewards shared equitably?

In addition to splitting tasks you will also benefit from having early conversations about how much ownership each person will have in the business. There are no hard rules about how much each person should own but the most popular format is an equal split. If you are a team of two and are equally committed to the business, a 50-50 ownership usually works well. You just need to make sure that you have a plan of action on how you will deal with gridlock (i.e. how do you make a decision when each 50-percent owner has a different view?).

In other cases the split of business ownership doesn't have to be exactly equal. In some situations entrepreneurs assign an *idea premium* to the individual who came up with the business concept. This can range from 10 to 15 percent.[5] Applying such a premium in a team of two means that the split of business ownership could be 60-40, in favour of the person who came up with the idea.

Action step 1: Co-founders

Lena has no experience building apps so she won't be able to launch her grocery delivery business without outside help. However, she's made a shortlist of potential people to work with. Here are some names. Have a read and see who you think would be a suitable co-founder.

- **Nelson** has been Lena's friend for many years. He also works in the telecoms industry but as a software developer. Lena and Nelson have similar interests and share lots of mutual friends and colleagues.
- **James** is an acquaintance who Lena worked with on a charity project during her gap year. He's developed a few apps in his spare time but currently works as a waiter at a local restaurant.
- **April** is Lena's best friend. She's more outgoing than Lena and currently works at an accounting firm. She's more risk averse but is very good with details and numbers.

Which of these candidates would you choose to work with? And how would you split the ownership of the business?

Step 2. Identify your customer

At this stage you will want to clarify your idea so that it is more tangible and executable. You will also want to focus your efforts with an effective launch strategy. This can be achieved by answering two questions: (1) who is your customer? (2) what is your unique selling proposition/point (USP)? Let's start with the customer.

Who is your customer?

In the chapters on marketing and strategy we came across the concept of focus. While it's important to maintain this view at every stage of entrepreneurship, it's especially vital when identifying the group of people you will market and sell your product to. This is because without a clear idea of who your customer is, you risk having mixed messages and straining resources as you attempt to please everyone. However, if you can focus on a particular customer you increase your chances of solving their problems and fulfilling their desires effectively. How can you identify your target customer?

The first thing you will want to do is to generate a list of all types of individuals who are likely to buy from you. If you are thinking of starting a videography business, for example, you may generate the following list:

- Corporate clients
  - Financial services businesses
  - Retail outlets
  - Dental practices
  - Charities
- Consumer clients
  - Musicians
  - Politicians
  - Newly married couples (weddings)
  - Motivational speakers

Next, you will want to narrow down your choices according to the following factors:

- **Buying power.** Can this group of people afford your services? Do they have sufficient disposable income?
- **Frequency of purchase.** How often will these individuals buy from you? Will they purchase things as a one-off or are they likely to make several purchases per year?
- **Access.** How easy is it to get access to this group of individuals? Are they within reach of your network or do you have to spend a lot of time and money to find them?
- **Urgency.** Do these individuals have a compelling reason to buy from you? How urgent are their problems and desires?
- **Competition.** How many businesses already cater to this group of individuals? What is the nature of the products and services already available? Do you have what it takes to compete?

Once you narrow your choices to a handful of customer groups (e.g. two to five) you can then conduct primary and secondary research to assess how attractive these groups are.

Primary Research: Primary research involves going out and talking to people who may find your product or service useful. It's important to do this before creating anything because when you speak to people you can learn things that will change your approach to the business. However, be careful not to initiate conversations with questions such as:

- 'Would you buy this product?'
- 'What do you think of my idea?'
- 'How much would you pay for this service?'

People will answer such questions hypothetically and in ways that are different from how they would answer if your product or service were available for purchase. Also, if you ask people what they think of your idea they will try to protect your ego by mincing what they really think. To have better research conversations, try adopting some of the following principles:[6]

- Listen more. Talk less.
- Adopt a curiosity mindset and ask open questions that don't presuppose the answer you are looking for.
- Ask questions about specific behaviours. For example, if you are thinking of starting a retail business focused on socks, you might ask, 'When's the last time you bought a pair of socks?', or 'What do you like or hate about the process?'
- Ask about current solutions. For example, you may ask, 'How are you currently solving problem X?' or 'How do you currently fulfil desire Y?'
- Ask about the implications of behaviours and solutions. For example, you may ask, 'What are the implications of doing X?', or 'What do you like or hate about Y?'

The point of speaking to people is to help you understand your target customers. And if you understand your customers you will design a better business for them. But if you speak to no one you won't know whether the problem you are solving is urgent enough. You also won't know what parts of a problem are more important to different groups of people. So before building your business, be sure to speak to at least 10–20 people so that you understand where your focus should be.

Secondary Research: Secondary research can complement your primary efforts with information that's readily available. For instance, if you are thinking of starting a craft beer business you can google 'craft beer sector' to learn about the changes in the market. Here are some things you will want to look out for:

- Is the market growing?
- Who are the top competitors in the area?
- Are there any gaps that the competition has missed?
- Is the market seasonal? For example, ice cream businesses do significantly better in the summer than in the winter.
- What are the latest innovations in the area? And will you be able to take advantage of them?

Knowing your target customer and market is critical so be sure to spend a few weeks or more learning about them.

 Action step 2: Target customer

Lena and her team have spent some time thinking about the target customer for their grocery delivery business. They have decided to focus on one particular group of customers. Their thinking process is detailed below.

- **Step a) brainstorm for target markets:** students, young families, graduates, professionals, pensioners, people in offices, construction site workers, school teachers
- **Step b) shortlist of potential target market:** graduates, students, young families, professionals who live in the city centre

Primary Research The team interviewed a sample of ten students, ten graduates, and ten young couples with families. The team learnt that graduates who lived in the city centre had the most sporadic grocery shopping habits. Even more interesting, recent graduates who worked in the financial services sector had the busiest lives but also the largest amount of disposable income.

Secondary Research Lena and the team decided to focus on 'graduates in the financial services sector and who live in the city centre'. A few *Google* searches also confirmed Lena's preference. She learnt that the financial sector was employing more graduates than ever and that now would be a great time to start a business that caters to this particular group. But what would be compelling to this target market? How can Lena and the team meet the needs of this group effectively? The team must now scrutinise the unique angle they will be taking with the business.

Step 3. Identify your unique selling proposition/point (USP)

Understanding your target customer helps with the articulation of benefits your business can offer in comparison to the status quo. Therefore, spend some time reflecting on the conversations you had during your market research. Try to pick out themes that can help you identify the most important benefits you can offer to your customers. These will be themes you can use to establish your USP.

At this stage it's also possible to employ one of the competitive business strategies discussed in Chapter 8 (i.e. cost leadership, differentiation, or focus). Alternatively, you can also reflect on the *benefit principles* discussed in Chapter 10. Whichever way the USP is crafted, try to keep it short and compelling.

 Action step 3: The USP

Lena and the team have decided to focus on the following type of customer: <u>recent graduates</u> who live in the <u>city centre</u>, and <u>work in the financial services</u> sector.

Notice how specific the profile is. This makes it easier to picture the kind of person Lena's business will cater to. It will also shape the marketing and sales strategy.

Thanks to the primary research Lena and the team conducted, they learnt that their target customer makes a good income, loves convenience, and subscribes to online film and music streaming services.

The team also learnt that although this person may be organised in the office, they are a bit disorganised at home. The team therefore see a great opportunity to position a premium grocery delivery business with the following USP:

Chapter 15

> **'Premium groceries delivered within 60 minutes.'**
>
> This value proposition sounds compelling but is it feasible? Lena and the team must now consider how to validate and launch the business without breaking the bank.

Step 4. Design a minimum viable product (or service)

Before committing to a business idea in full, you should first test how viable it is. This can be achieved by developing a compact version of your product or service in order to establish whether people will buy it and whether the business has potential to grow. Entrepreneurs commonly refer to this version of an offering as a minimum viable product.[7] It's a version of your idea that helps you test business viability with the least amount of resources. One of the pioneers of this concept, Eric Ries, suggests that when it comes to thinking about a minimum viable product, think of it as a cupcake rather than a large cake with half the ingredients missing.

Employing a minimum viable product strategy could save you months of work on an idea people might not necessarily want to pay for. But how exactly can you develop a more compact version of your business idea? Before we get to that, let's briefly look at the aims of developing a minimum viable product or service (the 'MVP'). These are:[8]

1. **To test your value proposition.** Will people pay for what your business has to offer? Surveys and market research can help but often the way people respond to surveys is different from how they act. An MVP can provide significantly better evidence.
2. **To establish how the business will grow.** Will your target group buy from you or will some other unexpected segment of the market buy more than you expected? How will your business grow from these early customers to larger markets?

An MVP should be designed with these questions in mind and once you launch your business, you will want to refer back to these questions to check you are on the right track. So what does an MVP look like? Here are some examples.

If you want to open a restaurant you could start with a food stall at food festival events. This route is cheaper and provides you with access to a lot of potential customers who can provide feedback on your menu.

If you want to build an online shop you could test the waters with trade on *eBay*. This way you can gauge demand without spending too much money on building a dedicated website.

And if you want to open a yoga studio, why not start by offering yoga classes in a local gym? This way you not only learn whether there's demand for yoga in your area, you also end up building relationships with people who might become your first customers when you open your own studio.

A MVP varies depending on the kind of business you hope to start. But in each case it's a version of your offering that can most effectively test whether enough people are willing to pay for your product or service.

 Action step 4: The minimum viable product (or service)

Lena and her team need to consider the most fundamental aspect of their business. Are people really willing to pay a premium to have groceries delivered within 60 minutes? If customers are not willing to pay for such a service and the business spends lots of money designing a mobile app, Lena and her team would have wasted a lot of resources for nothing. So it's better for the team to test the idea incrementally. Here's how they might start the venture with MVP principles in mind.

- **Limit deliveries to 7 p.m. to 12 a.m.** This is when people are back home from work.
- **Limit deliveries to Monday to Thursday.** Most people are out on Friday nights and a majority visit large supermarkets on the weekend for their main grocery needs anyway.
- **Don't build a mobile app yet.** Start with a simple website that takes orders with cash to be paid upon delivery. That way, you don't have to worry about processing debit or credit card transactions.
- **Limit the range of items on offer.** Start with a few items such as toiletries, pasta, drinks, salt, spices, and snacks.

That is just one MVP angle but it's possible to start with an even more minimal approach. For instance, Lena and her team could create a mock-up website with a registration page where people can enter their email addresses if they are interested in the service. The team could then print 200 cards with the website link and take them along to events that young finance professionals attend. The team can distribute these cards to people at the event and wait to see whether anyone signs up on the website.

Step 5. Write a five-page business plan

Business plans are a mixed bag in the realm of entrepreneurship. On one hand, practitioners and scholars argue that it's beneficial to write a business plan. This is because it helps you think about the future and the goals you hope to attain. A business plan can also help you communicate your ambition to co-founders and potential investors. However, during the early stages of a business, information is usually limited and there are far too many uncertainties. In this instance, business plans involve a lot of guesswork. Even worse, if you stick to them too rigidly you risk exposing yourself to emergent threats or missing out on unexpected opportunities. The following *insight box* is just one of many entrepreneur testaments to this fact.

> ## ⌘ Entrepreneur's Insight
> ## Erica Mackey, COO & co-founder of Off Grid Electric
>
> *The business plan and the business that we raised our initial funding for after leaving business school… the only thing that still holds true today is that it's the same market that we're addressing. So our model has significantly evolved as we've learnt more and as technology has become more available to enable what we do today.*

Despite the weaknesses of business plans there is still some value in planning ahead. Writing down your intentions helps you clarify your idea, goals, and allocation of time and money. In fact, research on business plans shows that they do contribute to enhanced business performance but that it depends on context.[9]

For a new venture, basic business planning is sufficient. This is because you will ideally be creating something new. You will also have less reliable information (until you have customers) and will face more uncertainty relative to an established business. For these reasons a simpler business plan (i.e. one that is five-pages long) is advantageous. You just have to stay flexible enough to respond to new opportunities and threats as you launch your venture.

Short business plan template

What does a good business plan look like? At the very least it should cover the basics of your business model, i.e. a plan of how you will create, deliver, and capture value.[10] This section will give you an idea of what else to include but feel free to amend your plan as you see fit.

Page 1

Who is your customer? This section should include information about your target customers. Who are they? Where are they? How many of them are there? What behaviours do they exhibit?

What is your value proposition? This section explains your USP while contrasting it with competitors in the marketplace.

How will you reach your customers? This section includes details on the following:

- How will you market your business?
- How will you facilitate word of mouth?
- How will customers buy from you?
- How will you support customers after they buy from you?

Page 2

How will you make money? How much will you charge customers? Will it be a payment per order or a subscription? Will prices be fixed or will you vary them according to some variable such as age or season of the year? This section will include all details on how you intend to make money.

Page 3

Start-up costs? If you need funding, how much do you have to raise to get your venture off the ground? How will it be spent?

Page 4

What does the future hold financially and operationally? How much money will you make? Where and how will you grow the business?

Page 5

Who's on the team and what are their responsibilities? What do you personally bring to the table in terms of experience, skills, expertise, and funding? Who are your co-founders and what are their roles and contributions?

A short business plan should be something for you and the team to refer to from time to time. If things change, update it. The document should not be static.

Once the business gets going you may be required to produce a more extensive business plan. Suggested readings are provided in the *Useful Resources* sections of this book but if you google 'business plan templates' you will also find lots of guidance in this area.

A word of caution, however; business plans should be written with a target audience in mind. Bankers, for example, place more emphasis on the financial aspects of the document. They prefer detailed financial information on how well your business is doing and what you expect to earn in the future. In contrast, investors such as those on *Dragons' Den* take a different approach. They place a larger emphasis on the background, experiences, and track record of the entrepreneur.[11] So keep the audience in mind when preparing a more detailed document.

 Action step 5: The business plan

Lena now has a MVP and is ready to launch. But before doing so it's time to produce a short business plan. Lena decides to write a draft that will be developed further with the help of her co-founders. Here are the bullet points she intends to use as starting points for her business plan:

- **Target customer:** 21–30 years old; works at a financial institution; lives in a city-centre apartment
- **Unique selling point / value proposition:** Premium groceries delivered within 60 minutes. We bring convenience and quality to busy lives.
- **Customer reach and distribution:** We will use social media marketing to reach our target customers. We will also attend

social events in the financial services sector. We will hire students to make deliveries.

- **Revenue model:** Customers pay for each order separately. But we will consider subscription models if they prove to be a popular demand.
- **Costs:** Our main costs include groceries, software development, and delivery activities. We currently don't need start-up cash and are using our savings.
- **Future goals:** We expect 175 orders per week in the first few months but hope to grow this to 700 within 18 months. We will expand our focus from finance professionals to include other professionals who work in demanding occupations (e.g. young doctors).
- **Team:** Lena works in the telecoms sector and is passionate about marketing. Her co-founders are equally skilled in other complementary areas.

Chapter 15

Step 6. Launch, refine, pivot

At this stage you will have a team, a clear target market, a value proposition, a minimum viable product or service, and hopefully a short business plan to guide you. You might now think that all that's left is for you to open your business to the public. However, designing your business doesn't stop on launch day. You must continue to refine your offering and adjust your strategy according to feedback.

Pay special attention to your first few customers. Their comments will be invaluable. They will tell you what works and what doesn't. Also, some customers will be very critical but try not to take it personally. Furthermore, other customers might be more timid in providing feedback but encourage them to offer suggestions on how you can make your product or service better. The key is to learn as much as you can before investing significantly in the business.

As you open up your venture to more customers you may also learn that your target market behaves differently to what you expected. Don't be put off by this. Expect many surprises and stay alert to any new opportunities (e.g. a new target market) or threats (e.g. a new competitor) that emerge.

 Action step 6: Launch, refine, pivot

Lena and the team successfully launch the premium grocery delivery business, offering a set of limited items at specific times in the week.

The team initially focused on young finance professionals. However, within the first few months they learn that almost anyone living in the city that is between the ages of 21 and 35 buys from them. This is a great opportunity to grow the business as long as the team refines the service before offering it to a wider audience.

Step 7. When to quit your day job

At the beginning of this book we learnt that entrepreneurship eventually becomes an all-in sport. This means that for your business to realise its fullest potential you have to commit to it wholeheartedly. But as a graduate it's likely that you will already have a day job. This presents conflict since you won't have as many hours to dedicate to your job or the business. Be that as it may, there are two ways to overcome this.

First, it's possible to develop and run your business in the evenings and on weekends. If you start small and employ a MVP approach, you will be able to test whether your idea is worth quitting your job for. You can also continue to run your business on the side until it generates enough income to replace your salary. This method applies especially well to businesses that do not require your presence on a 9 a.m. to 5 p.m. basis.

The second method involves planning for your business (but not actually running it just yet) while also saving funds that will enable you to fully immerse yourself in entrepreneurship for at least 12–18 months. This method is more suitable for business ideas that will require your presence on a 9 a.m. to 5 p.m. basis. It also requires more patience since you will have to save enough money to be able to go without a salary for a year or longer. But once you make that leap, you can focus 100 percent on growing your business while not worrying about rent or food.

 Action step 7: Quitting the day job

Since Lena and the team started with a limited service (deliveries between 7 p.m. and 12 a.m., Monday to Thursday), they were all able to work on the business while keeping their day jobs. They met on weekends to talk through business issues and had the rest of the week to implement solutions.

After three months of trade, Lena and the team learn that their venture is more viable than they had expected. They are already making more than 50 deliveries a week, with each order averaging £12. The business is generating sales of £600 each week and current projections show that this figure will quadruple within six months.

At this point, Lena and the team start planning when they will leave their jobs to pursue the venture full-time. But Lena is due for a promotion in a year so leaving her job isn't something she is going to take lightly.

⌘ **Entrepreneur's Insight**
Anthony Francis, co-founder and CEO of EventNinja

University graduate Anthony Francis managed to raise funding for his app business before he left his day job at *J.P. Morgan*. Along with his friends they built a software product that grew popular and attracted investment from an accelerator – an organisation that invests in entrepreneurs while offering an intensive business education and mentoring program. Anthony summarised this part of his journey as follows:

> *With the time I had we were able to leverage three people. So it was me and the two other co-founders and we managed to build a*

product on the side while I was working and while they were working in their organisations as well. We managed to get some traction and that enabled us to get into Oxygen Accelerator, which at the time offered €50,000 for 8 percent of the company.

Chapter summary

- There are no hard rules to follow when starting a business. Still, there are steps you can take to maximise your chances of building a successful venture.
- To increase your odds of success, get a co-founder (or two); be specific about your target customer; and make sure you have a strong USP.
- If a full-scale version of your business will cost a lot of money, start small instead and use the MVP approach.
- You don't need a detailed business plan when you start your venture. You just need a short document (five pages at most) that will clarify your plans and thoughts.
- When you finally launch your business, be open to feedback and be ready to pivot if customers pull you in a more profitable direction.
- Finally, don't quit your day job unless (1) you have enough money to go without income for 12–18 months, or (2) your business is making enough money to replace your salary or cover your basic income needs.

Useful resources

- Book: *Business Model Generation: A Handbook for Visionaries, Game Changers, and Challengers* (2010) by Alexander Osterwalder and Yves Pigneur

  Why is it worth reading?
  If you would like to create a detailed plan for your venture this book is a great place to start. It provides a business model template that has been used by thousands of entrepreneurs and is suitable for both small and large businesses.

Closing thoughts

In this book you've learnt that entrepreneurship is not as intimidating as it seems and that it's simply a process of identifying, evaluating, and exploiting opportunities. You've learnt that in order to do well you need an entrepreneurial mindset (self-belief, passion, endurance, creativity, leadership) and skill set (strategy, marketing, sales, branding, finance). In the final part of the book you also learnt how to find business ideas, how to evaluate opportunities, and how to make your venture a reality. What comes next?

Hopefully you've acquired a good foundation of business knowledge and can now confidently start working on your business idea in the real world. Of course there's still much to learn. But most of that learning will happen as you execute your idea in real life.

Also remember that the *Useful Resources* sections of this book offer guidance if you wish to explore specific topics in more detail. The learning never stops with entrepreneurship. And so, this book should mark not the end but rather the beginning of your personal transformation in business. Good luck!

*

For extra content visit www.palgravecareerskills.com

Notes

Introduction

1. Shane, S., 2009. The Illusions of Entrepreneurship: The Costly Myths That Entrepreneurs, Investors, and Policy Makers Live By, New Haven, CT: Yale University Press.

Chapter 1: The seven myths of entrepreneurship

1. Bhidé, A., 2000. The Origin and Evolution of New Businesses, New York: Oxford University Press.
2. Krentzman, J., 1997. The Force Behind the Nike Empire. Stanford Magazine. Available at: http://pgnet-saa.stanford.edu/get/page/magazine/article/?article_id=43087 [Accessed September 10, 2015].
3. Wadhwa, V. et al., 2009. Anatomy of an Entrepreneur: Family Background and Motivation. Kauffman Foundation Small Research Projects Research. Available at: http://www.kauffman.org/~/media/kauffman_org/research reports and covers/2009/07/anatomy_of_entre_071309_final.pdf [Accessed January 2, 2015].
4. Nianias, H., 2015. Zoella: YouTube Vlogger Buys Five-Bedroom Brighton Mansion Worth £1 Million. Available at: http://www.independent.co.uk/news/people/zoella-youtube-vlogger-buys-five-bedroom-brighton-mansion-worth-1million-10052939.html [Accessed April 23, 2015].
5. Stangler, D., Marion, E. & Spulber, D., 2013. The Age of the Entrepreneur: Demographics and Entrepreneurship. Innovation for Jobs. Available at: http://i4j.info/wp-content/uploads/2013/05/i4jDaneStanglerDemographicsandEntrepreneurship-1.pdf [Accessed April 14, 2016].
6. Shane, S., Locke, E. & Collins, C., 2003. Entrepreneurial Motivation. Human Resource Management Review, 13(2), pp. 257–279.

7. Hutcheson, J., 2007. The End of a 1,400-Year-Old Business. Businessweek. Available at: http://www.bloomberg.com/bw/stories/2007-04-16/the-end-of-a-1-400-year-old-business businessweek-business-news-stock-market-and-financial-advice [Accessed April 6, 2015].

8. De Geus, A., 2002. The Lifespan of a Company. Businessweek. Available at: http://www.businessweek.com/chapter/degeus.htm [Accessed April 6, 2015].

9. Coad, A. et al., 2013. Growth Paths and Survival Chances: An Application of Gambler's Ruin Theory. Journal of Business Venturing, 28(5), pp. 615–632.

10. See note 9.

11. Snyder, B., 2015. Vinod Khosla: Be Wary of 'Stupid Advice'. Insights by Stanford Business. Available at: https://www.gsb.stanford.edu/insights/vinod-khosla-be-wary-stupid-advice [Accessed July 17, 2015].

12. Torrance, J., 2013. Entrepreneurs Work 63% Longer than Average Workers. Real Business. Available at: http://realbusiness.co.uk/article/22838-entrepreneurs-work-63-longer-than-average-workers [Accessed November 10, 2015].

13. Rose, D., 2014. Angel Investing: The Gust Guide to Making Money and Having Fun Investing in Startups, Hoboken, NJ: John Wiley & Sons.

14. Graham, N., 2011. My First Million: Richard Reed of Innocent Drinks. Financial Times. Available at: http://www.ft.com/cms/s/0/e13793d4-a0ba-11e0-b14e-00144feabdc0.html [Accessed August 13, 2015].

15. Amorós, J. & Bosma, N., 2014. Global Entrepreneurship Monitor 2013 Global Report. Global Entrepreneurship Research Association. Available at: http://www.gemconsortium.org/report/48772 [Accessed November 17, 2015].

16. Guillebeau, C., 2012. The $100 Startup: Reinvent the Way You Make a Living, Do What You Love, and Create a New Future, New York: Crown Business.

Chapter 2: What is entrepreneurship?

1. Hébert, R. & Link, A., 2006. Historical Perspectives on the Entrepreneur. Foundations and Trends in Entrepreneurship, 2(4), pp. 261–408.

2. Casson, M. & Casson, C., 2013. The Entrepreneur in History, Basingstoke, UK: Palgrave Macmillan.
3. Van Doren, C., 1991. A History of Knowledge, New York: Ballantine Books.
4. Hudson, M., 2010. Entrepreneurs: From the Near Eastern Takeoff to the Roman Collapse. In The Invention of Enterprise: Entrepreneurship from Ancient Mesopotamia to Modern Times. Princeton, NJ: Princeton University Press, pp. 8–39.
5. Companies House, 2015. Register a Private Limited Company Online. Available at: https://www.gov.uk/register-a-company-online [Accessed November 27, 2016].
6. Ahmad, N. & Seymour, R., 2008. Defining Entrepreneurial Activity: Definitions Supporting Frameworks for Data Collection. OECD. Available at: http://www.oecd-ilibrary.org/economics/defining-entrepreneurial-activity_243164686763 [Accessed October 4, 2015].
7. Schumpeter, J., 1980. The Theory of Economic Development: An Inquiry into Profits, Capital, Credit, Interest, and the Business Cycle, New Brunswick, NJ: Transaction Publishers.

Chapter 3: Self-belief

1. PricewaterhouseCoopers, 2012. 15th Annual Global CEO Survey 2012, Available at: https://www.pwc.com/gx/en/ceo-survey/pdf/15th-global-pwc-ceo-survey.pdf [Accessed May 18, 2015].
2. Lowe, J., 2007. Warren Buffett Speaks: Wit and Wisdom from the World's Greatest Investor, Hoboken, NJ: John Wiley & Sons.
3. Amoruso, S., 2014. #Girlboss, New York: Penguin.
4. Fannin, R., 2008. How I Did It: Jack Ma, Alibaba.com. Inc.com. Available at: http://www.inc.com/magazine/20080101/how-i-did-it-jack-ma-alibaba.html [Accessed April 27, 2015].
5. Cooper, A. & Woo, C., 1988. Entrepreneurs' Perceived Chances for Success. Journal of Business Venturing, 3(2), pp. 97–108.
6. Karabegović, A. & McMahon, F., 2008. Economic Freedom of North America 2008. Economic Freedom Network. Available at: http://www.freetheworld.com/efna2008.html [Accessed May 26, 2015].

7. Hole, J., 1998. Interview: Frederick W. Smith. Academy of Achievement. Available at: http://www.achievement.org/autodoc/printmember/smi0int-1 [Accessed April 27, 2015].

8. Kinley, P., 2013. Air Cargo Freight, (n.p.): Clinton Gilkie.

9. Baron, R., 2013. Enhancing Entrepreneurial Excellence: Tools for Making the Possible Real, Cheltenham, UK: Edward Elgar.

10. Bandura, A. & Wood, R., 1989. Social Cognitive Theory of Organizational Management. Academy of Management Review, 14(3), pp. 361–384.

11. Cohen, W., 2013. The Practical Drucker: Applying the Wisdom of the World's Greatest Management Thinker, New York: Amacom.

12. Maddux, J., 2005. Self-efficacy: The Power of Believing You Can. In The Oxford Handbook of Positive Psychology. New York: Oxford University Press, pp. 277–287.

13. Bandura, A., 1994. Self Efficacy. In Encyclopedia of Human Behavior. New York: Academic Press, pp. 71–81.

14. Brooks, A., 2014. Get Excited: Reappraising Pre-Performance Anxiety as Excitement. Journal of Experimental Psychology, 143(3), pp. 1144–1158.

15. Burge, K., 2014. Performance Anxiety: Get Your Butterflies 'Flying in Formation'. ABC Health & Wellbeing. Available at: http://www.abc.net.au/health/thepulse/stories/2014/02/13/3944039.htm [Accessed December 12, 2015].

16. Greven, C. et al., 2009. More Than Just IQ: School Achievement Is Predicted by Self-Perceived Abilities—But for Genetic Rather Than Environmental Reasons. Psychological Science, 20(6), pp. 753–762.

17. Waaktaar, T. & Torgersen, S., 2013. Self-Efficacy Is Mainly Genetic, Not Learned: A Multiple-Rater Twin Study on the Causal Structure of General Self-Efficacy in Young People. Twin Research and Human Genetics, 16(3), pp. 651–660.

18. See note 10.

19. Carlson, N., 2012. Meet the 28-Year-Old Who Made $400 Million Today. Business Insider. Available at: http://www.businessinsider.com/meet-kevin-systrom-a-qa-the-28-year-old-who-just-sold-his-startup-to-facebook-for-1-billion-2012-4?IR=T [Accessed June 2, 2015].

Chapter 4: Passion

1. Todd, A., 2007. Vera Wang (Asian Americans of Achievement), New York: Chelsea House.
2. Bloomfield, L., 1984. Language, Chicago, IL: University of Chicago Press.
3. Rendich, F., 2014. Comparative Etymological Dictionary of Classical Indo-European Languages: Indo-European - Sanskrit - Greek - Latin, (n.p.): CreateSpace Independent Publishing.
4. Robinson, K. & Aronica, L., 2014. Finding Your Element: How to Discover Your Talents and Passions and Transform Your Life, New York: Penguin.
5. Vallerand, R., 2008. On the Psychology of Passion: In Search of What Makes People's Lives Most Worth Living. Canadian Psychology, 49(1), pp. 1–13.
6. Jobs, S., 2007. D5 Conference 2007. All Things D. Available at: http://allthingsd.com/20070531/d5-gates-jobs-transcript/ [Accessed April 13, 2016].
7. Cardon, M. & Kirk, C., 2013. Entrepreneurial Passion as Mediator of the Self-Efficacy to Persistence Relationship. Entrepreneurship: Theory and Practice, 39(5), pp. 1027–1050.
8. Mitteness, C. & Cardon, M., 2010. The Importance Angels Place on Passion when Making Investment Decisions: Why Does it Matter to Some and Not All Angels? Frontiers of Entrepreneurship Research, 30(2), pp. 44–57.
9. Vallerand, R., 2012. The Role of Passion in Sustainable Psychological Well-being. Psychology of Well-Being: Theory, Research and Practice, 2(1), pp. 1–21.
10. Vallerand, R. et al., 2010. On the Role of Passion for Work in Burnout: A Process Model. Journal of Personality, 78(1), pp. 289–312.
11. Chen, P., Ellsworth, P. & Norbert, S., 2015. Finding a Fit or Developing It: Implicit Theories about Achieving Passion for Work. Personality and Social Psychology Bulletin, 41(10), pp. 1411–1424.
12. See note 4.
13. Byrne, F., 2015. More Lives than One: The Extraordinary Life of Felix Dennis, London: Ebury Press.

14. See note 11.
15. Dennis, F., 2006. How to Get Rich, London: Ebury Press.
16. See note 15.

Chapter 5: Endurance

1. Hicks, A., 2012. Angie Hicks, Founder & CMO of Angie's List. Mariashriver.com. Available at: http://mariashriver.com/blog/2012/01/angie-hicks-founder-cmo-angies-list/ [Accessed July 21, 2015].
2. Taleb, N., 2007. Fooled by Randomness: The Hidden Role of Chance in Life and in the Markets, London: Penguin.
3. McClure, D., 2015. Lecture 1: How to Start a Startup. Genius.com. Available at: http://genius.com/4093579 [Accessed October 9, 2015].
4. Klein, G., 2007. Performing a Project Premortem. Harvard Business Review. Available at: https://hbr.org/2007/09/performing-a-project-premortem [Accessed October 9, 2015].
5. Beilock, S., 2011. Choke: The Secret to Performing Under Pressure, London: Constable.
6. Irvine, W., 2009. A Guide to the Good Life: The Ancient Art of Stoic Joy, New York: Oxford University Press.
7. Hirsch, J. et al., 2009. Optimistic Explanatory Style as a Moderator of the Association between Negative Life Events and Suicide Ideation. Crisis, 30(1), pp. 48–53.
8. Weil, F., Lee, M. & Shihadeh, E., 2012. The Burdens of Social Capital: How Socially-Involved People Dealt with Stress after Hurricane Katrina. Social Science Research, 41(1), pp. 110–119.
9. Isaacson, W., 2011. Steve Jobs: The Exclusive Biography, London: Abacus.

Chapter 6: Creativity

1. Johnson, S., 2010. Where Good Ideas Come From: The Natural History of Innovation, London: Penguin.
2. Palermo, E., 2014. Who Invented the Printing Press? Live Science. Available at: http://www.livescience.com/43639-who-invented-the-printing-press.html [Accessed November 9, 2015].

3. Konig, S., 2001. Cleaning Up in Business, With a Mop. New York Times. Available at: http://www.nytimes.com/2001/02/11/nyregion/cleaning-up-in-business-with-a-mop.html?pagewanted=all [Accessed November 9, 2015].

4. Byrnes, J., 2005. Nail Customer Service. HBS Working Knowledge. Available at: http://hbswk.hbs.edu/archive/4569.html [Accessed November 8, 2015].

5. Linderman, M., 2008. Defining the Problem of Elevator Waiting Times. Signal v. Noise. Available at: https://signalvnoise.com/posts/1244-defining-the-problem-of-elevator-waiting-times [Accessed November 8, 2015].

6. Scott, G., Leritz, L. & Mumford, M., 2004. The Effectiveness of Creativity Training: A Quantitative Review. Creativity Research Journal, 16(4), pp. 361–388.

7. Amabile, T., 1996. The Motivation for Creativity in Organizations. Harvard Business School. Available at: http://www.hbs.edu/faculty/Pages/item.aspx?num=13674 [Accessed November 8, 2015].

8. Catmull, E., 2014. Creativity, Inc.: Overcoming the Unseen Forces That Stand in the Way of True Inspiration, London: Bantam Press.

9. Melograni, P., 2006. Wolfgang Amadeus Mozart: A Biography, London: University of Chicago Press.

10. Barker, J., 1993. Paradigms: The Business of Discovering the Future, New York: Harper Business.

11. Simonton, D., 1997. Creative Productivity: A Predictive and Explanatory Model of Career Trajectories and Landmarks. Psychological Review, 104(1), pp. 66–89.

12. Jung, R. et al., 2015. Quantity Yields Quality When it Comes to Creativity: A Brain and Behavioral Test of the Equal-odds Rule. Frontiers in Psychology, 6(864), pp. 1–8.

13. Bayles, D. & Orland, T., 2001. Art & Fear: Observations on the Perils (and Rewards) of Artmaking, Eugene, OR: Image Continuum Press.

14. Ward, T., 2004. Cognition, Creativity, and Entrepreneurship. Journal of Business Venturing, 19(2), pp. 173–188.

15. Baron, R., 2013. Enhancing Entrepreneurial Excellence: Tools for Making the Possible Real, Cheltenham, UK: Edward Elgar.

16. Tharp, T., 2003. The Creative Habit: Learn It and Use It for Life, New York: Simon & Schuster.

17. Wallas, G., 1926. The Art of Thought, New York: Harcourt Brace.
18. Csikszentmihalyi, M., 2001. Creativity. In The MIT Encyclopedia of the Cognitive Sciences. Cambridge, MA: MIT Press, pp. 205–206.

Chapter 7: Leadership

1. Swift, M., 2011. Susan Wojcicki: The Most Important Googler You've Never Heard Of. San Jose Mercury News. Available at: http://www.mercurynews.com/business/ci_17286427 [Accessed September 14, 2015].
2. Laporte, N., 2014. Rebooting YouTube. Fast Company. Available at: http://www.fastcompany.com/3033534/innovation-agents/rebooting-youtube [Accessed September 14, 2015].
3. Northouse, P., 2013. Leadership: Theory and Practice, 6th ed., London: Sage Publications.
4. Cogliser, C. & Brigham, K., 2004. The Intersection of Leadership and Entrepreneurship: Mutual Lessons to Be Learned. Leadership Quarterly, 15(6), pp. 771–799.
5. Kabendera, E., 2015. How Tanzania Plans to Light up a Million Homes with Solar Power. The Guardian. Available at: http://www.theguardian.com/environment/2015/oct/29/how-tanzania-plans-to-light-up-a-million-homes-with-solar-power [Accessed March 1, 2016].
6. Kouzes, J. & Posner, B., 1987. The Leadership Challenge: How to Get Extraordinary Things Done in Organizations, San Francisco, CA: Jossey-Bass.
7. Baum, R., Lock, E. & Kirkpatrick, S., 1998. A Longitudinal Study of the Relation of Vision and Vision Communication to Venture Growth in Entrepreneurial Firms. Journal of Applied Psychology, 83(1), pp. 43–54.
8. BBC. Mission and Values. Available at: http://www.bbc.co.uk/corporate2/insidethebbc/whoweare/mission_and_values [Accessed November 14, 2015].
9. Hogan, R. & Kaiser, R., 2005. What We Know About Leadership. Review of General Psychology, 9(2), pp. 169–180.
10. Harrison, J., 2014. When We Were Small: Ben & Jerry's. Washington Post. Available at: https://www.washingtonpost.com/business/on-small-business/when-we-were-small-ben-and-jerrys/2014/05/14/069b6cae-dac4-11e3-8009-71de85b9c527_story.html [Accessed November 15, 2015].

Chapter 8: Strategy

1. Greene, R., 2007. The 33 Strategies Of War, London: Profile Books.
2. De Wit, B. & Meyer, R., 2010. Strategy: Process, Content, Context: An International Perspective, Andover: Cengage Learning.
3. Ronda-Pupo, G. & Guerras-Martin, L., 2012. Dynamics of the Evolution of the Strategy Concept 1962–2008: A Co-word Analysis. Strategic Management Journal, 33(2), pp. 162–188.
4. Hitt, M. et al., 2001. Guest Editor's Introduction to the Special Issue Strategic Entrepreneurship. Strategic Management Journal, 22(6-7), pp. 479–491.
5. Freedman, L., 2013. Strategy: A History, New York: Oxford University Press.
6. Nohria, N., Joyce, W. & Roberson, B., 2003. 4+2 = Sustained Business Success. HBS Working Knowledge. Available at: http://hbswk.hbs.edu/item/42-sustained-business-success [Accessed August 22, 2015].
7. Porter, M., 1996. What is Strategy? Harvard Business Review, 74(6), pp. 61–78.
8. Stevenson, S., 2013. We're No. 2! We're No. 2! Slate.com. Available at: http://www.slate.com/articles/business/rivalries/2013/08/hertz_vs_avis_advertising_wars_how_an_ad_firm_made_a_virtue_out_of_second.html [Accessed November 24, 2015].
9. Biciunaite, A., 2013. Redefining the 'Lipstick Effect'– Examples of Recession-Proof Categories. Euromonitor International. Available at: http://blog.euromonitor.com/2013/11/redefining-the-lipstick-effect-examples-of-recession-proof-categories.html [Accessed July 24, 2015].
10. Barnouw, J., 2004. Odysseus, Hero of Practical Intelligence: Deliberation and Signs in Homer's Odyssey, Lanham, MD: University Press of America.
11. Bruder, J., 2012. A 13-Year-Old Enlists M.B.A. Students to Build Her Start-Up. New York Times. Available at: http://boss.blogs.nytimes.com/2012/05/01/a-13-year-old-enlists-m-b-a-students-to-build-her-start-up/ [Accessed November 24, 2015].
12. Rumelt, R., 2011. Good Strategy/Bad Strategy: The Difference and Why it Matters, London: Profile Books.

13. Porter, M. E., 1980. Competitive Advantage: Techniques for Analyzing Industries and Competitors, New York: The Free Press.
14. Gadiesh, O. & Gilbert, J., 2001. Transforming Corner-Office Strategy into Frontline Action. Harvard Business Review, 79(5), pp. 72–79.

Chapter 9: Marketing

1. Mercedes-Benz, 2014. Bertha Benz: A Woman Moves the World. Available at: https://www.mercedes-benz.com/en/mercedes-benz/classic/bertha-benz/ [Accessed May 5, 2015].
2. Erickson, B., 2006. The Woman Behind the Man: Bertha Benz and the First Automobile. UAW Chrysler. Available at: http://www.uaw-chrysler.com/images/news/firstcar.htm [Accessed May 6, 2015].
3. Boucher, E., 2011. Mercedes-Benz Museum: The Automobile as a Work of Art. Michelin.com. Available at: http://travel.michelin.com/web/destination/Germany-Stuttgart/news-Mercedes_Benz_Museum_the_automobile_as_a_work_of_art-MercedesstraSSe_100 [Accessed May 6, 2015].
4. Daimler, 2008. August 1888: Bertha Benz Takes World's First Long-Distance Trip in an Automobile. Daimler. Available at: http://media.daimler.com/marsMediaSite/en/instance/ko/August-1888-Bertha-Benz-takes-worlds-first-long-distance-tri.xhtml?oid=9361401 [Accessed May 6, 2015].
5. Frankel, A., 2013. Bertha Benz — the Mother of Motoring. Telegraph. Available at: http://www.telegraph.co.uk/motoring/10275540/Bertha-Benz-the-mother-of-motoring.html [Accessed May 6, 2015].
6. Kotler, P. & Armstrong, G., 2014. Principles of Marketing, 15th ed., Harlow, UK: Pearson Education.
7. Moore, G., 1991. Crossing the Chasm: Marketing and Selling Disruptive Products to Mainstream Customers, New York: Harper Collins.
8. ONS, 2015a. Families and Households: 2015. Statistical Bulletin. Available at: http://www.ons.gov.uk/peoplepopulationandcommunity/birthsdeathsandmarriages/families/bulletins/familiesandhouseholds/2015-11-05/pdf [Accessed March 1, 2016].
9. See note 7.

10. See note 7.
11. Godin, S., 2005. Purple Cow: Transform Your Business by Being Remarkable, London: Penguin.
12. Ries, A. & Trout, J., 1994. The 22 Immutable Laws of Marketing, London: Profile Books.
13. Berger, J., 2013. Contagious: How to Build Word of Mouth in the Digital Age, London: Simon & Schuster.
14. Barwise, P. & Meehan, S., 2010. The One Thing You Must Get Right When Building a Brand. Harvard Business Review. Available at: https://hbr.org/2010/12/the-one-thing-you-must-get-right-when-building-a-brand [Accessed November 7, 2015].

Chapter 10: Sales

1. ONS, 2015b. Release: Labour Force Survey Employment status by occupation, April - June 2015. Available at: http://www.ons.gov.uk/ons/rel/lms/labour-force-survey-employment-status-by-occupation/april---june-2015/2015-spreadsheet.xls [Accessed November 22, 2015].
2. Pink, D., 2014. To Sell is Human: The Surprising Truth About Persuading, Convincing, and Influencing Others, Edinburgh: Canongate Books.
3. Fredrickson, B., 2013. Positive Emotions Broaden and Build. Advances in Experimental Social Psychology, 47(1), pp. 1–53.
4. See note 2.
5. Fredrickson, B. & Losada, M., 2005. Positive Affect and the Complex Dynamics of Human Flourishing. American Psychologist, 60(7), pp. 678–686.
6. Etherington, B., 2008. Selling Skills for Complete Amateurs, London: Marshall Cavendish.
7. White, R., 1977. The Entrepreneur's Manual, Radnor, PA: Nelson Canada Limited.
8. Kaufman, J., 2012. The Personal MBA: A World-Class Business Education in a Single Volume, London: Penguin.
9. See note 8.
10. Grant, A., 2013. Rethinking the Extraverted Sales Ideal: The Ambivert Advantage. Psychological Science, 24(6), pp. 1024–1030.
11. See note 2.

Chapter 11: Branding

1. Blake, P., 2011. Before Surnames. BBC. Available at: http://www.bbc.co.uk/history/familyhistory/get_started/surnames_01.shtml [Accessed March 1, 2016].
2. Alter, A. & Oppenheimer, D., 2006. Predicting Short-Term Stock Fluctuations by Using Processing Fluency. Proceedings of the National Academy of Sciences, 103(24), pp. 9369–9372.

Chapter 12: Finance

1. Branson, R., 2009. Losing My Virginity, London: Virgin Books.
2. Branson, R., 2012. Virgin's Richard Branson Bares His Business 'Secrets'. NPR. Available at: http://www.npr.org/2012/10/10/162587389/virgins-richard-branson-bares-his-business-secrets [Accessed November 11, 2015].
3. See note 2.
4. Kaufman, J., 2012. The Personal MBA: A World-Class Business Education in a Single Volume, London: Penguin.

Chapter 13: Identifying Opportunities

1. Dyer, J., Gregersen, H. & Christensen, C., 2008. Entrepreneur Behaviors, Opportunity Recognition, and the Origins of Innovative Ventures. Strategic Entrepreneurship Journal, 2(4), pp. 317–388.
2. Graham, P., 2012. How to Get Startup Ideas. Paulgraham.com. Available at: http://paulgraham.com/startupideas.html [Accessed December 1, 2015].
3. Farzan, A., 2015. The Fabulous Life of Spanx Billionaire Sara Blakely. Business Insider. Available at: http://uk.businessinsider.com/the-fabulous-life-of-spanx-billionaire-sara-blakely-2015-5 [Accessed August 15, 2015].
4. Pandya-Wagh, K., 2015. The 21-Year-Old Building India's Largest Hotel Network. BBC. Available at: http://www.bbc.co.uk/news/business-34078529 [Accessed October 23, 2015].
5. Linkner, J., 2012. Is Your Company Selling Aspirin, or Vitamins? Fast Company. Available at: http://www.fastcompany.com/1826271/your-company-selling-aspirin-or-vitamins [Accessed November 23, 2015].

6. Reiss, S., 2002. Who am I? 16 Basic Desires that Motivate Our Actions Define Our Personalities, New York: Berkley Publishing.

Chapter 14: Evaluating opportunities

1. Shane, S., 2009. The Illusions of Entrepreneurship: The Costly Myths That Entrepreneurs, Investors, and Policy Makers Live By, New Haven, CT: Yale University Press.
2. Schlossberg, M., 2015. The Fastest-Growing Gym in America has $10 Memberships and Gives out Free Pizza, Bagels, and Candy. Business Insider. Available at: http://www.businessinsider.com/planet-fitnesss-business-profile-2015-10 [Accessed January 13, 2016].
3. Ernst & Young, 2015. Venture Capital Insights - 4Q14. Global VC Investment Landscape. Available at: http://www.ey.com/Publication/vwLUAssets/Venture_Capital_Insights_4Q14_-_January_2015/$FILE/ey-venture-capital-insights-4Q14.pdf [Accessed December 4, 2015].
4. Sarasvathy, S., 2001. What Makes Entrepreneurs Entrepreneurial? Effectuation.org. Available at: http://www.effectuation.org/sites/default/files/research_papers/what-makes-entrepreneurs-entrepreneurial-sarasvathy_0.pdf [Accessed May 11, 2015].
5. Hindle, K., 2004. A Practical Strategy for Discovering, Evaluating, and Exploiting Entrepreneurial Opportunities: Research-Based Action Guidelines. Journal of Small Business & Entrepreneurship, 17(4), pp. 267–276.
6. Thiel, P. & Masters, B., 2014. Zero to One: Notes on Start Ups, or How to Build the Future, London: Penguin.

Chapter 15: Exploiting opportunities

1. Aulet, B., 2013. Disciplined Entrepreneurship: 24 Steps to a Successful Startup, Hoboken, NJ: John Wiley & Sons.
2. Wasserman, N., 2013. The Founder's Dilemmas: Anticipating and Avoiding the Pitfalls That Can Sink a Startup, Princeton, NJ: Princeton University Press.
3. Kolodny, L., 2013. How Solo Founders Beat The Odds and Get Into Top Accelerators. Wall Street Journal. Available at: http://blogs.wsj.com/venturecapital/2013/03/12/how-solo-founders-beat-the-odds-and-get-into-top-accelerators/ [Accessed November 14, 2015].

4. Roberts, E., 1991. Entrepreneurs in High Technology : Lessons from MIT and Beyond, New York: Oxford University Press.

5. See note 2.

6. Fitzpatrick, R., 2013. The Mom Test: How to Talk to Customers & Learn if Your Business is a Good Idea When Everyone is Lying to You, (n.p.): CreateSpace Independent Publishing Platform.

7. Ries, E., 2011. The Lean Startup: How Constant Innovation Creates Radically Successful Businesses, London: Penguin.

8. See note 7.

9. Brinckmann, J., Grichnik, D. & Kapsa, D., 2010. Should Entrepreneurs Plan or Just Storm the Castle? A Meta-analysis on Contextual Factors Impacting the Business Planning–performance Relationship in Small Firms. Journal of Business Venturing, 25(1), pp. 24–40.

10. Osterwalder, A. & Pigneur, Y., 2010. Business Model Generation: A Handbook for Visionaries, Game Changers, and Challengers, Hoboken, NJ: John Wiley & Sons.

11. Mason, C. & Stark, M., 2004. What do Investors Look for in a Business Plan? International Small Business Journal, 22(3), pp. 227–248.

Index

Your Notes

Your Notes

Your Notes

Your Notes

Your Notes